Battle in the Irish Sea

The Life and Death of HMS Manners

David Gibson

*Catholic priest,
the last Baronet of Great Warley
and former A/S Officer*

MARITIME BOOKS

*To those who served with Royal Naval Escort
and Support Groups, especially our Shipmates
who did not come home.*

*First published in 1993 by
Maritime Books, Lodge Hill,
Liskeard, Cornwall, U.K.*

ISBN 0 9521432 0 8

*Typeset and printed in Great Britain by
Penwell Ltd, Callington, Cornwall.*

Contents

DE 523 is named HMS Manners. Mrs Fischer, Sarah Lawton, Lieutenant Jermain.

(Photo: Ldg Telegraphist A. Russell Stewart)

Foreword

In my address at the Commissioning Service of HMS *Manners* in Boston Navy Yard, I referred to an engagement that took place between a frigate commanded by Captain Lord Manners and a similar ship of the United States Navy not far from Land's End during the American Civil War of Independence.

My listeners were surprised that I should mention this, but I was able to mollify them by bringing out the point that the action was renowned for the exceptional courage shown by both ships who continued to fight until each had suffered forty deaths, an unusually high figure for frigates of that time. I expressed my hope that HMS *Manners* would live up to the tradition of him whose name we carried to sea and his adversary.

Little did I realise that, a year later, we would suffer casualties of the same order and that I would be able to report with pride of the courage and steadfastness shown by a crew who, though young, responded to the leadership of mature and experienced senior ratings.

As Father Gibson brings out, *Manners* was a happy ship, largely because she was an efficient ship. She had her difficult moments, but, as Admiral Sir Max Horton remarked during one of my carpetings, her sins were those of commission and not of omission and he would always forgive the former.

Father Gibson has done a great service, not only in recording the life of HMS *Manners*, but also in setting her operational view in the context of the closing stages of the Battle of the Atlantic when the action became a more individual one between a new generation of submarines manned by crews of undeniable courage and the escorts and aircraft who hunted them. Although we managed to contain the threat there was a worry that new and faster submarines might regain the initiative. We at sea, however, had confidence that the developing tactics with new equipment and a growing co-operation between escorts and aircraft would prevail.

One of my happiest memories is of the warmth and the hospitality shown to us by the lady who named the ship, Sara, Mrs. Fischer. I am in regular touch with her family whom she imbued with her rather eccentric but highly cultured charm and doggedness. It includes, for example, a Judge whose hobby is hang-gliding and his son who is a ballet dancer of world acclaim. I often feel that Mrs. Fischer's character was woven into the spirit of her ship which responded so courageously in the day of her adversity.

Captain Denis Jermain, DSC., RN
Pipers' Pool,
Petersfield.

CHAPTER ONE

A Ship is Commissioned

The World War of 1939 to 1946 was still at its height during the course of 1944. Great tonnages of shipping were being sunk by enemy submarines, especially in the North Atlantic Ocean. It was here that packs of up to ten U Boats working together, awaited the passing convoy. All merchant shipping moved in convoy, being in constant need of protection by the smaller types of warships. These destroyers, frigates, corvettes and converted peacetime fishing trawlers were aided, sometimes, by Aircraft carriers and even the occasional capital ship but, normally, they voyaged back and forth across the seas unaided by the Big Guns. To muster large numbers of loaded shipping into correct positions within the convoy needed signals by light as use of radio could be used by the enemy to identify the locality.

DE 523 was initiated as a destroyer escort on 14th August, 1943 at the Boston Navy Yard in Massachusetts for this specialised task of convoying. Designed by American Naval Architects to British specifications as a mass produced replacement for Royal Naval war losses,the design was adopted and expanded by the United States Navy as a result of the growing threat to them of being drawn into the war. The class was to be powered by diesel electric or steam turbine, of 1,085 tons, with a length of 289'6", a beam of 35' and a draft of 8'3". They were armed with three 3" guns and four Oerlekons. Six thousand horse power was produced by eight sixteen cylinder diesels which turned four main generators these in turn, powering the two main propulsion units. A propeller shaft speed of 750 revolutions gave her a speed of 18½ knots. Assembly of the ships involved many different yards but the final welding of all these together took but two or three weeks.

She was a pretty ship, possessing a fine lined bow and a shapely sheer along an unbroken main deck. It was rumoured that the Boston Yard had designed the Destroyer escorts with all the diesels in one water tight compartment, the generators in the next and the two propulsion units in the third. This rumour had the Royal Navy asking the obvious question, *'What happens if one of those compartments is flooded?'* It is inconceivable that the Navy Yard should have designed such a marvellous vessel and yet have built into it such a serious flaw. However accurate the rumour, it remained true that the Destroyer Escorts were received by the Royal Navy with some of each of these vital machines in separate compartments so that if holed in one, the ship could still manoeuvre.

The launching ceremony was performed by Mrs. Fischer, the wife of the Boston Navy Yard's Chief Constructor, Captain Hugo Fischer, USN. The bottle of Brut Champagne was smashed on the stem of the new ship with the traditional words of naming, *"I name this ship, Manners, may God be with her and all who sail in her."* Captain Hugo stood by with Miss June Lawton, Lady in Waiting, and our own Lieutenant Denis Jermain, RN, the new Commanding Officer.

The transfer of DE 523 to the United Kingdom took place on 16th December, 1943, being commissioned by the Royal Navy on that same day as one of the Captain Class Frigates, all of which carried the name of one of the Captains of the Line who had served at the Battle of Trafalgar. DE 523 was named after Lord Robert Manners, who was born in the year 1758 to become one of Lord Nelson's Captains. He commanded HMS *Resolution* at Trafalgar but fell, mortally wounded at the Battle of the Saintes. On both bows of *Manners* was painted her new Royal Naval number, K-568.

During the four days after commissioning, the new ship received her full complement of crew. Lieutenant Denis Jermain, RN Commanding Officer, Lieutenant Braithwaite, who, a few months later on receiving his own command, was replaced by Lieutenant J.C. Carter as First Lieutenant Royal Naval Volunteer Reserve, Lieutenant J. Walker of the Royal New Zealand Navy, who, later in 1944 gave place to Lieutenant Frank Collett, RNVR, Lieutenant (E) E. Riches, Royal Naval Reserve Engineer, Lieutenant Adams, RN Navigator, Lieutenant D.W. Collins RNVR, Gunnery Officer, Sub Lieutenant David Gibson RNVR, Asdic Officer and Sub Lieutenant George Glynn RNVR as Staff Officer, together with ninety two crew members.

This crew was complete by 24th December and the next day, Christmas Day, our commissioning was commemorated on the Quarter deck by our Commanding Officer, Lieutenant Jermain, with a Service of prayer and Christmas carols. This service, for which we stood in snow several inches deep, was attended on the quayside by some fifty members of the Dockyard labour force. They were aware of the purpose for which the ship had been built, a purpose summed up succinctly in the official wording of Naval history, *"During World War II, Manners served on patrol and escort duties in the North Atlantic, protecting the vital flow of men and material first to England, and after D. Day, to the continent, enabling Allied fighting men to wrest Fortress Europa from Hitler's armies and save mankind from the Nazi scourge."*

As 'fitting out' had not been completed, '*Manners*' remained alongside for ten days, during which time, we added to our inventory by touring the dockyard and chalking our Yard Number, DE 523, on the required articles. Next day, a dockers' work party would arrive to fit and test the item. For instance, the United States Navy did not permit any inflammable materials in their ships, resulting in no carpet in cabins and wardroom – just a bare steel deck, painted red. In our dockyard perambulations, we found great rolls of carpeting which we inscribed with 'DE 523.' This was fitted throughout the ship.

Our Commanding Officer recalls with amusement *"That the pace of building activity was exemplified by the manner in which gangs*

*of welders (all of whom were female) would patrol the ship at night,
looking for fittings to be welded into place, indicated by chalk
marks saying, 'Weld here.' During the embarkation of ammunition,
the depth charges had been left on deck overnight. Each British
depth charge has a stencilled sign reading, 'Weld here' indicating
the join in the casing where the two parts meet. The inevitable happened and the next morning, we found all our depth charges firmly
welded to the upper deck."*

'*Manners*' was a welded ship without a rivet in her entire length.
The feeling among all of us was that, in the event of a torpedo striking the hull, every seam would open up immediately and we would
sink far more quickly than a dose of salts. But experience, just one
year later, was to prove us wrong !

Lt. Braithwaite liked to tell the story supposed to have taken place
during the storing of the new ship. He put in a requisition for knives
and forks and spoons and an extra one for fish knives and forks. The
Replenishment form, signed by him, was correct in all details:-

> *Knives. Fish. 10. To replenish.*
> *Forks. Fish. 10. To replenish.*

Twice, the requisition form came back '*Not granted*,' as a result of
which and as a last resort, Lt. Braithwaite placed the third order
form:-

> '*Ten fish knives and forks to eat fish with.*'

The Wardroom certainly had these implements on board by sailing date!

The gathering of that one hundred strong crew had taken place
over the past three months. I had been serving in HMS *Wrestler*
which had seen eminent service in the Great War. In that ancient
'V' and 'W' destroyer, we had assisted in the peaceful occupation of
the Azores Islands doing so at the invitation of Portugal with whom
Great Britain had a long standing Treaty. Army personnel, their
stores and all the equipment needed for the creation of an aero-
drome were landed with some difficulty on the Island of Terceria.
This difficulty arose as a result of petrol being loaded in the bottom

of ships' holds so that the entire cargo had to be off loaded on prim-
itive quay areas before the lorries could be started. This task took
four or five weeks. For us in *Wrestler*, the return voyage was with a
convoy of aging iron ore carriers from Freetown to the United
Kingdom. The maximum speed of this convoy was a mere four
knots, slow enough for submarines to keep up while submerged.
One ship only was lost after being struck by a torpedo which had
passed a few feet ahead of *Wrestler*'s bow. Laden with iron ore, she
sank like a stone, so quickly that two survivors only were picked out
of the sea, one of whom had been asleep in his bunk two decks
down, awakening in the sea!

A new appointment awaited me on arrival in Glasgow; I was to
take passage to Newfoundland in HMCS *Arvida*. This seven hundred and fifty ton vessel was a Flower Class Corvette, though she
lost her 'Flower' name in transfer to the Royal Canadian Navy. A
Lieutenant Newcome was appointed also to take passage to St.
John's though the phrase, 'To take passage' did not mean a cruise
for us, rather a working interlude in order to take up new postings
in America. The voyage across the Atlantic took twelve days with
some forty ships in company. The weather was not too severe, but
bad enough to prove that corvettes were capable of rolling badly,
even, as her crew insisted, on wet grass! The voyage was without
incident and the convoy was delivered safely to the Escort group
taking them on to New York and other destinations.

St. John's, in November, is cold and foggy, with ice in the harbour
and snow on the bare mountains, but the warmth of its reception
was marvellous. Ashore, I meet up with a Mr. Paddon who seemed
eager to obtain a few hand grenades, *"Could I oblige?"* On request-
ing the reason for this petition, he said, *"Oh, I'm not taking over the
Government, I want them for night fishing."* The idea being to sight
a good fish with the aid of torch light and then to drop a grenade
some ten feet away from it. This would stun the fish which was
then lifted out. The reason for this barbaric method of fishing the
Newfoundland rivers was a severe shortage of salmon fly. I

promised to bring some over on my next trip, keeping this promise
the following year on *Manners*' first visit to St. John's, buying in
Glasgow and swopping the salmon fly for nylon stockings, then
unknown in England.

After eight days in port, *Arvida* was due to sail home with the
next convoy. Lieutenant Newcome and I disembarked and walked
down the quay to the gangway of SS *Fort Amehurst*, a ten thousand
ton passenger liner bound for New York. Some twenty Officers were
already on board and we sailed that night. We called at Halifax in
Nova Scotia, being allowed ashore for an evening. Snow was very
deep and icicles very long, especially on the wooden building
which had caught fire, the water from hoses freezing almost as soon
as it left the nozzles.

Fort Amehurst entered New York Harbour at six in the morning, a
time giving just enough light to reveal the outline of the Statue of
Liberty against a backdrop of blazing lights. Coming from blacked-
out England – where to show the glimmer of a match was against
war-time law – this profusion of light struck us as almost miraculous. We tied up at one of the Cunard Piers and took a taxi to the
Barbazon Plaza Hotel on 42nd Street. The entire fifth floor of this
five star Block had been taken over by the Admiralty to serve as a
transit camp for those awaiting ships.

During the morning of December 23rd, I found my way to the
cathedral-like building of New York's Central Station where I board-
ed a train for Boston, about two hundred and fifty miles to the
north. Buying a newspaper for the journey, I was concerned to read
the headline, 'British sailors steal American Battleship.' but this
concern was mitigated on reading that the warship in question was
a small model on display in a toy shop. After one night as guest in
the American Wardroom at Fargo Barracks in the Dockyard, I joined
HMS *Manners* the next day, Christmas Eve.

'Fitting out' was declared complete as soon as our Royal Naval
Number, 'K 568' was painted on port and starboard bows.
Thereafter, we were ready for our maiden voyage. This took us one

(Photo: MOD)

HMS *Manners* at anchor in Grassy Bay, Bermuda.

hundred and fifty miles up the coast of New Hampshire and Maine to Casco Bay where we were to complete the calibration adjustments to compasses, the master gyro and the testing of degausing equipment.

Most of the wartime service of Lieutenant Jermain had been in motor torpedo boats. Others, faced with a sudden change to larger and more powerful vessels, might have found the prospect daunting, needing time to acclimatise to the fact that when 'full astern' was ordered nothing happened for some seconds whereas in MTBs, 'full astern' resulted almost as soon as the order was given. Our Commanding Officer did not get that time to adjust at leisure. On entering Boston Harbour at the end of the first day of sea trials, the harbour pilot who had taken Manners to sea seemed to lose his nerve on returning. Due to a strong cross current, he refused to take the ship into the very limited space allotted. The USN Captain who had come to supervise the trials told Lieutenant Jermain to take over and to get in at all costs.

As a result, and for the very first time he had handled the ship, our Skipper decided that the only way in which to handle the matter was to treat the new vessel as an MTB and enter with verve and at speed. Those watching from a US destroyer in the berth ahead were seen to run for their lives as the brand new ship headed straight for them, proudly showing a sizeable bow wave!

However, a touch of full astern got us alongside and the US Captain and the white-faced pilot were kind enough to congratulate the English Lieutenant. It could be that this event began the reputation of Lieutenant Denis – which apparently followed him for the next twenty five years – that he did everything at full speed! But it did work!

For our short stay in Casco Bay, the weather was so bitterly cold that to touch metal with a bare hand meant instant frostbite. I think we measured a temperature of 40° below zero. Snow seemed to have obliterated the town and stopped all movement within the harbour. The ship, however, was settling down beautifully, all of it worked, including the luxury unknown in most ships: heated air ventilation! On the morning on which we sailed for Bermuda, about nine hundred miles away, two of the crew did get frostbite while handling the anchor chain but, less than twenty four hours later, the thermometer was showing 80°F. with a very real risk of sunburn. The change had come very quickly as we passed from the cold Labrador current flowing from the north into the blue water, Gulf Stream.

Manners remained for one month based at Grassy Bay in Bermuda. Five other new Destroyer Escorts were in company, all of them given this time in safe waters to work up the anti-submarine team and the organisation of a new crew. We practised on friendly submarines, testing out our ability to find one, home onto it and attack it. The newest Asdics sets had been fitted in a very snug compartment ahead of the top bridge. Petty Officer Foster was the Higher Submarine Detector and there were four operators. These were Leading Seaman F.J. Bragg, S.D., Able Seaman B. Beeby S.D., Able Seaman J.C. McIntosh, S.D. and Able Seaman J. Jones, S.D. I was in charge of this anti-submarine team. Unlike the old hand operated 123. Asdic sets, our model included a recorder which showed every contact with objects under water, an electrically trained oscillator and a loudspeaker with a repeater on the bridge. Furthermore, there was a second oscillator which worked out the trigonometrical problem of range versus depth. *Manners* was among the first Naval ships to be fitted with the PPI (Plan Position Indicator) Radar set which was to revolutionise the war against the submarine. From then on, we were able to see a surfaced enemy submarine well before he could see us, this fact being especially useful at nightime or in bad visibility.

Manners left Bermuda in early March, 1944, homeward bound while undertaking our first convoy duties. The first ten days of that crossing were uneventful, having made a good rendezvous with the thirty ships we were to escort, we set a course for the southerly route across the Atlantic. Weather was fair, though the visibility became poor, and then bad. In the Bay of Biscay, our port propeller shaft sheered suddenly and for no apparent reason. The port engines had to be shut down. The shaft, together with its 'A' bracket and the propeller, seemed to be intact and still with us but no longer coupled to the union, just exterior to the hull. The convoy proceeded on its course, leaving us to limp home at slow speed. For the first time in our lives, we became thankful for the presence of thick fog, our radar screen informing us of German aeroplanes passing overhead but unable to see the 'sitting duck' beneath them.

The reason for this damage to the propeller shaft was the distance between the stern gland (where the shaft leaves the hull) and the 'A' bracket was too great, thus allowing 'whip' in the shaft. An extra bracket was fitted during the Birkenhead refit to give the necessary stiffness.

Manners began to feel safe after passing Tuskar Rock Lighthouse at the entrance to the Irish Channel. A dry-dock awaited us in Birkenhead and it was decided to make the visit a time for major refit. The vessel had proved to be too heavy below the water line, as a result of which, our first three thousand mile voyage proved conclusively that our new ship was almost as good at rolling as any Corvette. We suffered about thirty thousand rolls of forty five degrees or more. Our rolling time was six seconds. This meant that it took just six seconds to roll from upright, forty five degrees to starboard, forty five degrees to port, ending at upright once more. Our tablecloth was invariably well wetted in an effort to stop the plates sliding up and down the table!

Admiralty Fleet Orders entitled us to a twenty seven feet Naval Whaler to augment our lifesaving gear. The Ship required an extra pair of davits on which to hang this desirable boat. The Dockyard labour force repaired the propeller shaft and altered our rolling time from six to nine seconds by installing extra depth charge racks on the main deck. This raised the centre of gravity, which gave us a roll slightly better than any British destroyer.

D Day intervened during the two months of our dry docking, an event in which we would have shared had it not been for the loss of our propeller shaft. The crew consoled themselves by spinning yarns to their girl friends. These involved the most hair-raising tales of how we, alone, were winning through. Perhaps, the best of these was told by one of my anti-submariners. When asked what his Asdic badge was, he replied, *"Don't spread it about in case the enemy has ears, but I dive over the ship's side with a pot of green paint. Then, waiting for the periscope to show, I paint it green and rejoin the ship."* "But why," said the girl, *"Ah, the sub doesn't know that it has broken surface and we wait until he is about three hundred feet up and then shoot him down with anti-aircraft guns. We have shot down dozens!"*

At this time of the War, the mid-summer of 1944, hundreds of thousands of American Servicemen crammed every single nook and cranny of the land, all of whom were awaiting the chance to cross the Channel and commence the last stage of Hitler's war. The enormous logistical problem of landing vast numbers of Allied Forces on the beaches of Normandy was concluded successfully although the initial stages meant that, for some ten days or more, the invasion was a matter of touch and go. The weather did not help, being so unpromising on 'D' Day that the crossing was delayed twenty four hours, taking place on 'D' Day plus one. Troops already loaded in Landing Ships had to be unloaded again, this causing great anxiety in matters of security. Had the delay been longer than a day, the entire invasion would have been put back until the next Spring tides. The actual crossing of the Channel was in Force Four to Six weather. Squashed in small boats, the Army must have found those hours at sea almost unendurable, made worse by seasickness and the nervous tension of knowing not what to expect on arrival.

All of us in *Manners* in dry dock were aware of what was happening throughout the length of the English Channel, feeling keenly our inability to add our bit to the odds. Several Destroyer Escorts took part in the landings and the subsequent protection of ships carrying troops and armour to the beaches, Mulberry Harbours and

Cherbourg, the first large harbour to fall to Allied Forces. Some of these were lost or severely damaged. K 514, HMS *Lawford* was lost. Under the command of Lieutenant Commander Morris, she was serving as one of the HQ ships on Juno Beach between Arromanche and Carantan. At 0450 on the 8th June, 1944. She was attacked by German aircraft and sunk with heavy casualties. At 0315 on the 11th June, HMS *Halstead*, K 566, was damaged by German Torpedo boats off the Normandy beaches, again with heavy casualties. K 313, HMS *Blackwood* was sunk by U Boat 984 to the south east of Portland Bill but casualties were slight. On the 25th June, not quite three weeks into the Battle for Normandy, HMS *Goodson*, K 480 was torpedoed by U Boat 984 to the south east of Start Point but, with light casualties, managed to reach a home port. K. 575, HMS *Trollope* received from a Torpedo Boat light casualties and damage while on submarine patrol off Cap d'Antifer, twenty five miles north of Le Havre.

Two other Destroyer Escorts served as H.Q. Ships on the Normandy Beaches. These were the *Kingsmill* of which Lieut G.H. Cook was the Commander and the *Dacres* commanded by Lieut Commander G.C. Juliens, RNZVR.

Other losses occurred after the initial onslaught of the 'D' Day Beaches. On Boxing Day of that year, just off Cap de la Hague the same submarine, U Boat 486. inflicted heavy casualties on K 470, HMS *Capel* at 1237 and, fifteen minutes later, light casualties on K 462, HMS *Affleck*.

But such losses were, by no means, one sided: *Affleck* managed to sink U Boat 358 and U Boat 392, both of these off the Azores during the March of 1944. U Boat 1191 was sunk by her in the English Channel on 25th June, 1944. K 353, HMS *Essington* sank U Boat 988 in the Channel on 29th June. On the same day, K 466, HMS *Bickerton* managed to sink U Boat 269 off the coast of Normandy. In the subsequent three months, four more U Boats were sunk adjacent to the Beaches, these being U Boats 672, 212, 214, 671, all by Captain Class Frigates; *Balfour*, *Curzon*, *Cooke* and *Styner*. The total number of U Boats sunk by Captain Class Frigates during the war years was thirty five for the loss of ten frigates. Nelson, surely, would have been very proud indeed of this record, completed by ships named after his Captains and operated by young, sometimes very young, crews. Such sacrifices should not be forgotten by any subsequent generation of British people.

CHAPTER TWO

Seven months of Escort Duties

M*anners* was ready once more for sea in June, some days after 'D' Day. We took the ship to Campbeltown for an Anti-submarine 'work up.' Our sparring partners on the attack tables were members of the team from Captain Walker's famed ship, HMS *Starling*. He was the Senior Officer of the 'Support Group' which sank nineteen submarines during the course of the war. It soon became apparent that when his team obeyed the rules, the team from *Manners* were by far the better and more successful. He complained that, on contacting a submarine, it was his practice to clear the Asdic office of everyone excepting his Asdic Officer and the Petty Officer, Higher Submarine Detector, the two of them alone operating the sets until a 'kill' was obtained or the attack abandoned. At Campbeltown, he was not allowed to use this method.

'B2' Escort Group, of which we became a member, was engaged on the convoying of merchant shipping in the area of the North Atlantic. This work involved a crossing time of ten to twelve days each way, a turn round of about a week, usually in St. John's in Newfoundland, a week in Gladstone Dock at Liverpool and a three or four day 'work up' at Larne. A round trip, therefore, took about six weeks. Our Group Leader was HMS *Highlander*, a two thousand tonner known to us affectionately as *The Tribal Class Destroyer*. Her Commanding Officer was Captain J.V. Waterhouse, RN and the ship carried a Surgeon Commander.

On two occasions, while escorting a convoy, contact was established with a submarine. Captain Walker heard the ships of B2

Group talking to each other by TBS (Talk between Ships) Radio. He broke in on our conversation, ordering us to rejoin our convoy and he would take over the attack on our contact. His score of submarine 'kills' went up – ours remained the same! However, this was an eminently sensible way of acting in view of our own priority being the safety of ships which could not be left without defence.

Our anti-submarine 'work-up' completed, *Manners* sailed for the Minches between Scotland and the Hebridian Islands, in which waters Coastal Command Aircraft had sighted several periscopes. Very carefully, we patrolled through the one hundred and fifty miles of the South Minch, the Little Minch and the North Minch, doing this in the most beautiful weather, warm sunshine and halcyon breezes, but without seeing a single periscope. However, what we did see were dozens of basking shark fins and we assumed that it was these which had been reported by Coastal Command. We anchored for the night in Loch Eribol on the very northern coast of Scotland, continuing our search to the east along the coast as far as Dunnet Head, before returning through the Minches to Larne in Northern Ireland. From this port, we met up with other ships of 'B2' group, spending four days on exercises before joining Convoy ON. 260 bound for various parts of the States. Something like eighty cargo vessels had to be shepherded into place at the rendezvous just to the north of Rathlin Isle. Position 'A' was allocated to *Manners* this being two thousand five hundred yards ahead of the port column of the convoy. HMS *Mounsey*, our sister ship, was five thousand yards to starboard and we were unable to see the far side of the convoy. Three Norwegian Corvettes kept station astern of the convoy, about eight thousand yards behind us. Weather conditions were fair and we settled down to a speed of about ten knots.

No enemy action was observed throughout the eleven day voyage and we began to anticipate a pleasant eight day rest in St. John's. At 12.30 during the penultimate night before our arrival in Newfoundland, *Manners* shuddered when the engines were put 'full astern.' I did not get up from a warm bed as, suffering the effects of flu, I had left the bridge at 12.10, at the end of my watch. However, ten minutes later, the same thing happened again and then came the crash! Alarm bells sounded, I dived into some warm clothing and headed up ladders to the bridge so fast that the blood left my head and I felt dizzy. But wrapped round our bows was one of the Norwegian Corvettes, HMS *Rose*, and in the moonlight, it was obvious that we had crashed into the engine room.

It took twenty minutes for Rose to sink in position 45°50N. 40°15W. The date was 26th October, 1944, our thirteenth day out after sailing on Friday 13th! The final plunge was in a near vertical position with her bow high in the air. All hands, except two on watch in the engine room, were picked out of the water without injury. John McCourt, a member of the crew of HMS *Highlander*, assisted the survivors to board his ship. He remains very appreciative of the efficiency and discipline displayed by the Norwegians as they abandoned *Rose*. The boilers and depth charges were made safe and, once over the side, they kept physical contact with one another, ensuring that no one drifted away. Lieutenant Collins, RNVR, who had taken over the watch from me less than thirty minutes before, said that the Corvette had come from the port side and, therefore, was the 'giving way' ship, turning across our bows on both occasions. The first of these proved to be a near miss but, on the second try, it was impossible to miss. Our own bows were smashed back fifteen feet or more, but the rest of the ship remained watertight. The Damage Control team closed up, shored up the watertight bulkhead, making us safe for slow speeds, and we set a course for St. John's prior to the convoy being handed over to the Atlantic coast Escorts, based on Halifax.

The inevitable Courts Martial took place in Liverpool; the Norwegians were unable to account for being out of station by about eight or nine miles and, as far as we were concerned, *Manners* had always been in the correct place. It seemed to us, therefore, that, because a Norwegian ship was involved, Lieutenant Collins had to take the rap. He was reprimanded, which seemed to us unfair although this reprimand could have been as a result of not calling the Commanding Officer after the first near miss.

To repair the damage to our bows, we moved down the coast to Bay Bulls, a tiny hamlet of a town which boasted a slip large enough to haul us out of the water. There, such excellent work followed that, in eight days, we were shipshape and ready to meet our homeward bound convoy. It was on this occasion that I had brought over from Scotland a quantity of salmon fly, this being swopped for a large salmon – which I froze and stored in the ship's refrigerator – and a pile of nylon stockings. The voyage home, again, proved uneventful and after delivering some sixty ships to the Local Escort Group, we did what no ship before us had accomplished: we entered Liverpool in a pea souper of a fog, doing this by the aid of our Radar. The buoys on either side of the channel were clearly visible on the radar screen and it was reasonably easy to con the ship between them for the whole of the ten miles of channel. The first land seen as it loomed out of the fog was the sea wall of Gladstone Dock, some twenty feet ahead of our bows. The merchant ships – all without Radar – had to remain at anchor for a further week when fog cleared sufficiently for them to enter the various docks in the River Mersey.

It was on this occasion that we found RMS *Queen Mary* in the Gladstone dry dock under repair. At something like twenty five knots, she had sliced in two her escorting cruiser, HMS *Curacao*. Her bows were forced back about seventy feet by the impact and several hundred from the crew of *Curacoa* were lost in the sinking. It would seem probable that *Curacao* had altered course the wrong way at the end of the first hour of a two hour zig-zag.

Half the Ship's Company received seven days leave which enabled me to catch a train for Cornwall, together with my salmon, frozen solid and wrapped in many sheets of paper to keep it so for as long as possible. Plymouth, through which the train passed, had suffered, since my last visit; four days of very heavy bombing destroyed the city centre and the casualties had been especially

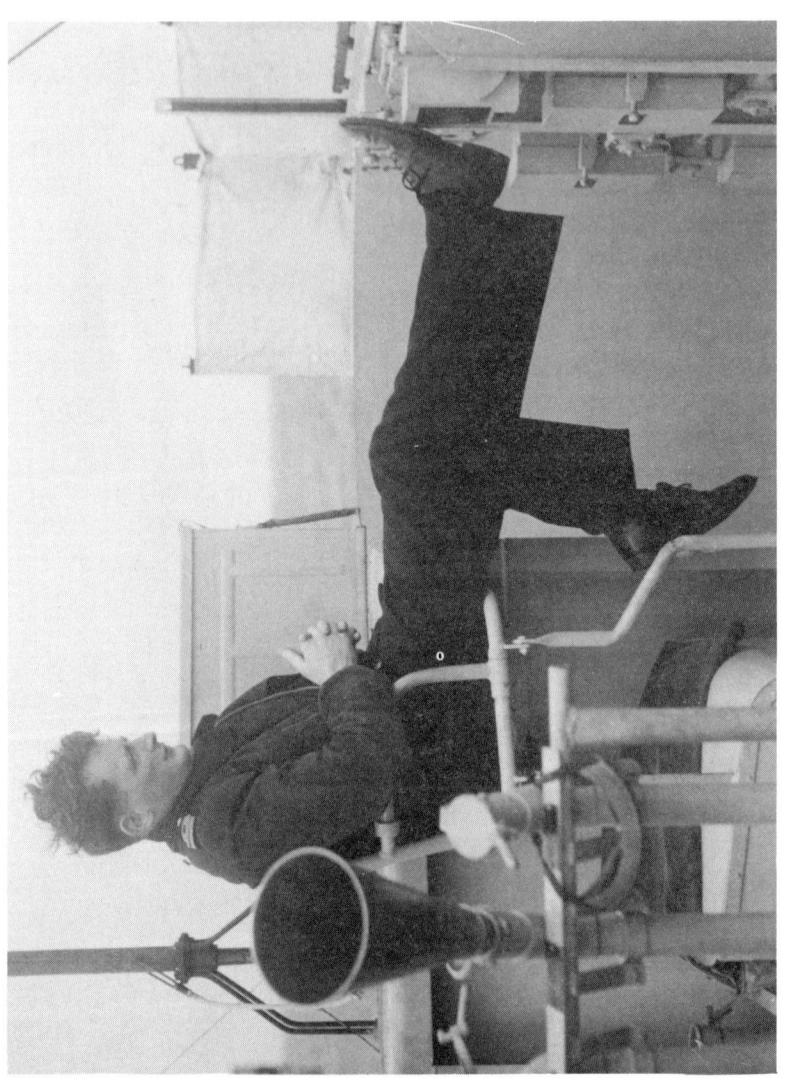

Our Commanding Officer, Denis Jermain, waits for the next thing to happen! Port side of the Bridge, North Atlantic.

(Photo: Capt D. Jermain.DSC, RN)

high. The entire City Centre from Drake's Circus to the Continental Hotel was one enormous heap of rubble. St Andrew's Church had been burnt out, the walls alone surviving. Our own Cathedral of St. Boniface had been saved from similar fate by the agility of Monsignor Jeremiah Ryan who, in spite of 'full habit,' popped up ladders and scrambled across tiles, pitching burning incendiary bombs into the void below him. The picturesque warren of old streets around the Guildhall had disappeared but many of the shops nearby, even though badly damaged, displayed the proud sign, 'Business as usual' and life seemed to be stoical in its refusal to give up.

After eating the whole of my salmon – en famille – I returned to Liverpool in time to sail with a 'UK to Italy, fast convoy.' Some twenty five troop transports and cargo vessels required escorts to Naples which had fallen to General Alexander's efforts to push back Kesselring's Tenth and Fourteenth German Armies. Salerno had been occupied by our Forces and the break-out from the landing site was advancing to Monte Cassino. A further landing on the beach at Anzio was being contemplated. Our convoy was to reinforce the success of that great man, General Alex. He had enabled our Eighth Army and the American Fifth Army to bring about victory in North Africa and the foot of Italy.

It was a measure of overall success in the war that our convoy received not one attack throughout its voyage to Gibraltar and along the coast of Morocco, Algeria and Libya. Even when all our ships turned to pass to the north of Sicily, not a single enemy plane was seen. During our approach to Naples, Vesuvius was erupting, its column of smoke giving us early clue to the direction of our destination. On arrival in Naples harbour, we manoeuvred into a quayside berth between two large cargo vessels. This caused the Italian Harbour Master to greet us with Latin apoplexy. A lot of arm waving, jumping on the spot and very expressionate language indicated to us that we were forbidden that particular berth. Leading Seamen Bragg, handling mooring wires on the f'castle, replied with quiet English candour, *"S'olright, Mate, we won."* As he spoke, he heaved a line at the 'gold-plated' uniform, proceeding to tie up. We discovered later that the berth was for the harbour master's personal motor launch, absent at the time as a result of 'war damage.'

Naples was a shambles, the civilian population suffering from food shortages and the failure of essential services. In spite of the absence of street lighting and the possibility that enemy snipers could still be lurking in ruined buildings, some of us decided to brave an evening ashore. We walked together to the Scala Opera House where a woman of full habit was to entertain. Her mezzo soprano voice certainly did that, she was marvellous. However, at the beginning of the Second Act, the lighting failed. The music continued, gradually fading out as more and more members of the orchestra failed to read the music. Finally, Madame continued alone, right to the end of the Act, after which we all walked home. The town seemed filled with begging children, orphans who had lost parents in the bombing and shelling – unless, of course, their parents had trained them for the job in order to survive.

Manners was fortunate in being given an anchorage on the other side of the Bay at Pozzuoli. No shore leave could be granted as it was still possible to meet up with a German sniper. But the view of Capri to the south of us and Vesuvius to the east, the volcano glowing at night, and the legendary Mediterranean sunshine kept us contented. Italy, at the time of our visit, had surrendered, the civilian people often looking upon us as liberators who were in process of driving the German Tenth and Fourteenth Armies out of their country. The morale of Kesselring's forces must have been low, knowing that it was a question of time only before they were pushed over the Alps.

Our return to Liverpool was as uneventful as the voyage out but our arrival meant a profound and providential change to the crew. Surgeon Lieutenant Michael Charles Connell, RNVR joined the Wardroom. A quick turn around in Gladstone Dock, enabled us to sail for our next voyage to Newfoundland. We sailed up the Irish

Sea to assemble a large convoy and its escorts off Rathlin Isle. It was the first convoy of one hundred ships to cross the Atlantic. In worsening weather, a lot of shepherding was necessary, but by nightfall, the entire fleet was on course with a speed of about ten knots. However, the weather continued to worsen, all the way up to Force 12. It took eight days to travel four hundred and fifty miles, during which time the largest and smallest were battered by seas of up to sixty feet in height and travelling at seventy or eighty miles an hour. Look-outs had to be withdrawn from 'B' Gun deck because of the very real danger of being swept overboard, together with the gun. The top bridge where, in the open air, Officers of the watch, for four hours at a time, tried to keep warm and dry, was forty five feet above the water line. However, on one occasion, this bridge was filled to waist height with water, the weight of which rolled us to within a few feet of sea level. On the ninth day, the sun broke through and the wind slackened considerably. There was but one ship in sight and it took all the daylight hours to contact twenty four others.

On one occasion, we caught up with a line of six or seven ships, heading south. By signal lamp, we asked the rear ship, *"What convoy are you?"* Back came the reply, *"UK to Halifax, following the next ahead."* Each ship in turn gave the same reply until we caught up with the leader. Its reply was, *"UK to Mediterranean."* This meant that we had to unscramble the rearward ships, give them a new course by which to regain the safety of their own Convoy and shepherd them northwest again. In between times, we added to the interest of the task by devising a method of measuring the heights of waves. If this method was accurate, we gauged two passing seas in excess of eighty feet. A magnificent and unforgettable sight!

Christmas Day 1944 was spent at sea on the homeward bound voyage. It was calm, very calm for the Atlantic in winter and it was, therefore, possible to celebrate the Feast in a relaxed and peaceful manner. Someone produced a large Christmas tree – no doubt purloined in the forest outside St. John's – and this was erected and decorated on the top bridge. Leading Stoker 'Tubby' Matthews, suitably clothed in red, with a cotton wool beard supplied by the Doctor, complete with bulging sack, took his seat on the roof above the Asdic Office as Father Christmas. With these festal decorations, we cruised among the ships of the convoy, conveying the greetings of the Season by means of our ship's choir doing their best on 'B' Gun deck with the aid of the loud hailer and well known carols. Ronald Bloomfield recalls this *"lovely day"* with deep feeling, remembering his part in the singing to the waving seamen who lined the rails of the merchant ships, so large as to make us feel rather small.

On the 30th. December, we reached Gladstone Dock. Next day, I was received into the Catholic Church, becoming thereby, the Senior Catholic on board, and on the 1st. January, Stoker First Class Ronald Bloomfield was married. On the 5th of January, leave was curtailed in order to meet up with a convoy to the south of Ireland. We were to assist in its safe escort through the Dover Strait to the Thames.

Part of our task was to separate the Liverpool and Glasgow sections of this convoy, forming a new convoy which would proceed up the Irish Sea to their destinations in the north. The remaining ships would then be escorted up the English Channel. *Manners* entered Falmouth Harbour and at anchor, was struck by an erring dredger moored ahead of us. A gale blew up and the dredger dragged down on us. The bucket gear, which projected over the stern like two sharp battering rams, punctured our bows before we could get clear. Although not seriously damaged, we had to enter dry dock for repairs. *Manners* was placed in dry dock for the third time in her short history. Repair took longer than expected and it was not until the 25th of January that we were pronounced fit to proceed to sea.

During the period in commission, *Manners* had completed four eastbound crossings of the Atlantic and three westbound making a total distance run of 20,000 nautical sea miles. Our return voyage through the Minches added about 1,200 miles more and the round trip to Naples a further 6,000, making almost 30,000 miles in the seven months of our duty. I think the Pitometre Log registered 32,000 miles at the end.

On the morning of our departure from Falmouth, I was able to organise a trip ashore for the sixteen Catholics on board. By motorboat, we landed in Falmouth and made our way to the Parish Church of the Immaculate Conception in Killigrew Street. Canon Fanning was the Parish Priest at that time and he was kind enough to hear the Confession of all sixteen and to arrange for a Mass to be said. All of us received Holy Communion before returning to the ship. We sailed for Liverpool at 1600 hrs, destined never to reach that port!

CHAPTER THREE

Battle in the Irish Sea

Germany produced a new type of torpedo during the course of 1943. It was an acoustic weapon, being homed onto a ship by propeller noises. This weapon became known to us as the Gnat Torpedo. Each type of ship has its own propeller noise signature, often so distinctive that, picked up by hydrophone, it is possible to identify the ship. Early in 1944, it was noticed that many ships were being damaged in the stern and that propellers were always blown apart.

Naval Research teams came up with the Foxer. Two metal bars some two feet long and held rigid with a small gap between them. Towed through water, some two hundred yards behind the ship. These bars vibrated, making more noise than the ship's propellers. At first, two of these Foxers were towed, entailing much encumbrance and operating difficulties if a depth charge attack became necessary. The homing torpedo was supposed to pick up first one foxer and then the other so that a figure of eight was made until fuel ran out and the torpedo either sank or exploded astern of the towing vessel.

The design was simplified a little by the Unifoxer towed directly astern. The torpedo would home onto this appliance, hopefully drifting off into empty water until fuel was expended and the torpedo either sank or exploded so far astern as to do no damage. *Manners* had been fitted with 'Foxers' during a previous visit to Liverpool. The Scientist who had overseen the installation, had written in our 'Visitors Book' *"May the Foxers fox 'em."*

For the final stages of the U Boat campaign, the idea of groups of U Boats hunting convoys in the North Atlantic seemed to be abandoned. Instead, submarines began to operate alone and near the coasts of Britain on known convoy routes. Convoys were coming across the Atlantic unmolested, only to meet trouble within sight of land. U Boats had certainly penetrated the minefields on either side of both entrances to the Irish Sea. They were also laying mines adjacent to navigational buoys and in shipping lanes in the English Channel. As a result, ships were being picked off and torpedoed or mined when least expecting attack.

It could be that the change in German submarine policy began with trial runs to the north and south of the Irish Sea in the November of 1944. U 483 managed to torpedo HMS *Whittaker* to the north of Malin Head on 1st November 1944. Casualties were very high and not one officer survived. The Fifth Escort Group received the SOS signal when it was in the Atlantic as a support group. The call for help read, *"Severely damaged, no officer survives. Chief Petty Officer in charge."*

Whittaker – one of our sister ships – had been escorting Convoy SC 159 just to the north of Lough Swilly in position 53° 30'N 07° 39'W. The torpedo hit in the engine room but detonated the hedgehog magazine, destroying everything forrard of the bridge and inflicting ninety two casualties in a complement of about one hundred men. The wreck was towed first to Moville by the tug *Earner* and then to Belfast.

Bligh was detached in order to proceed to *Whittaker*'s aid at full speed. Tom Kennie takes up the story, *"On arrival at the wreck just to the north of Malin Head we found* Whittaker *afloat in a calm sea. Our motor boat was dropped and an officer and four volunteers left* Bligh *to board.* Whittaker *had been hit amidships, her funnel was doubled over and the rear of the bridge was lying wide open and oil was spilling all around her. The motor boat came back to collect a roll of canvas, sailmakers' needles and string with which to sew up the dead bodies. Burning oil had done the worst damage to the crew in the after section of the vessel.*

Whittaker, *escorted by* Bligh, *was towed by tug into Belfast. On arrival,* Bligh *went alongside and, in view of the refusal of dockyard workers to assist, volunteers were asked to go aboard and help in the clearing up of the bodies. Other ships assisted us and everyone of the volunteers were taken to the Fleet canteen and given all the drink they wanted. Some of the young lads were crying their eyes out as the whole of the bridge area seemed to contain nothing but arms and legs protruding from the wreckage, these bits and pieces, of course, belonging to people we knew and with whom we had worked."*

A member of *Aylmer*'s crew, Dick Roberts, passed along the quay where *Whittaker* was moored and what he saw made him remark, *"The front part was wrapped around the bridge and hands, legs and bodies were hanging everywhere."*

Eventually, *Whittaker* was towed to Larne Harbour where she was broken up for scrap. One remains profoundly grateful to those volunteers from *Bligh* and all who undertook the gruesome work. At least, the remains were removed with care and reverently by people who knew them. U 483 managed to get home to Bergen undamaged. After hostilities ended, however, it was towed into the Atlantic and sunk in deep water by the British Operation Deadlight.

Between the 9th and 11th of January, 1945 it became obvious to the Western Approaches Headquarters in Liver Building in Liverpool that at least six U Boats were operating between Milford Haven and the Clyde. The American freighter, *Jonas Lie* of 7,198 tons and in Convoy ON 277 was torpedoed in 51°45N. 05°27'W., about seventeen miles from Milford. The trawler, *Huddersfield Town* took off her crew. Next day, the wreck had drifted to within thirty miles of Lundy Isle and tugs and escorts were sent to intercept. *Storm King* took her in tow but the last tow rope parted on the 12th January and the vessel was last seen off the Scillies and was thought to have sunk in heavy weather during that night .

On the evening of 11th January, two more ships were torpedoed to the west of Holyhead. These were the British *Normandy Coast* of

1,428 tons which sank at 1520 and the American *Roanoke* of 2,606 tons at 1536. Sixty seven survivors were brought safely into Holyhead by PC 74. and the *Senga* a Yugoslav vessel.

Lt. Commander Graf Matuschka in U 482 was not so fortunate as his opposite number in U 483. Captain Walker's Support Group, *Starling*, *Peacock*, and *Hart* attacked and sank this U Boat between the Mull of Kintyre and Islay in position 55°30'N 05°53'W. Commander Matuschka had attempted entrance into the Irish Sea after a highly successful voyage from Norway to the west coast of Scotland. U 482 was fitted with a schnorkel which more easily escaped surface detection, perhaps imparting a false sense of security to a successful crew. In the late summer of 1944, he had sunk the American tanker, MS *Jacksonville*, the corvette, HMS *Hurst Castle*, the MS *Pinto* and the British steamer *Empire Heritage*. At the beginning of this final voyage through the North Channel, Commander Matuschka had managed to destroy the Norwegian tanker, *Spinanger* and on the 15th January, 1945. at the entrance to the River Clyde, the auxiliary Aircraft Carrier, HMS *Thane* was torpedoed and so severely damaged as to be declared non repairable. The Carrier was taken in tow by the frigate *Loring* which managed to get the stricken vessel to Greenock by the 16th January. Ten of the crew of *Thane* were killed.

On that day, 16th January, U 482 was detected and sunk without survivor by Captain Walker's Support Group, *Starling*, *Peacock* and *Hart*. This sinking took place on the northern side of the North Channel position 55°30'N 05°53'W, about midway between the Argyle peninsula and Islay. The torpedoing of *Thane* marked the beginning of the U Boat offensive within the confines of the Irish Sea and in the inshore waters around the coast of Cornwall. In the next few weeks, no less that sixteen U Boats with all their crews were to be lost. The conflict seemed to end with the torpedoing of HMS *Teme* off Falmouth on the 29th March, 1945, this being the last fling prior to the ending of the War in Europe less than two months later.

At the southern end of the Irish Sea, several U Boats looked over

HMS *Manners* awaits the next convoy, at anchor in Larne.

(Photo: Sub. Lt. David Gibson, RNVR)

ways through the minefields and strung themselves across the known merchant ship routes. On 17th. December, U 400 was sunk by HMS *Nyasaland* just to the south of Ireland in position 51°16'N 08°05'W.

Nyasaland's final attack was dramatic. Mindful of the convoy safety, she had been ordered to rejoin after one last attack. She ran in at seven knots on a U Boat estimated to be at 200 feet. The enemy used evasive tactics but contact was held and a hedgehog pattern was fired at 2358. Eight and a half seconds after the projectiles entered the water, several detonations were heard followed almost immediately by an extremely violent explosion which lifted *Nyasaland* in the water. The target was regained astern at 200 yards when three echoes were heard but which faded away rapidly. Oil rose to the surface and the pungent smell of diesel oil was noticed. *Nyasaland* rejoined the convoy.

A little further to the west, although still off the south coast of Ireland, U 1200 met a similar fate by the attack of HMS *Pevensey Castle* aided by *Launceston Castle*, *Portchester Castle* and *Kenilworth Castle*.

To counteract these enemy activities, our own minelaying commenced in the English Channel during December, 1944. These were deep laid mines to ensnare the submerged U Boat operating along the south coast of England. Two troop transports, *Leopoldville* and *Empire Javelin* and two escorting frigates, *Affleck* and *Capel* were torpedoed. These new mines were deep laid in the vicinity of navigational buoys still at their normal peace time moorings. The minelayer *Plover* which had been at work off the south coast of Ireland was recalled to Portsmouth and began work with four Motor Torpedo Boats of the 64th Flotilla numbers 724, 728, 739, and 787, these being re-equipped for minelaying work.

These five vessels laid 1,152 mines in twenty voyages of Operation Brazier between the Isle of Wight, Cherbourg and Le Harve. It was not until late January that this activity was extended into the Irish Sea. HMS *Bligh*, before detaching to assist *Manners* during the morning of the 26th of the month, had been escorting the large mine-layer, HMS *Apollo* along the west coast of Wales.

The World War II Review, issue no. 15 tells us that Submariners have to be secretive in order to succeed in peace or war. Their motto is *Venio non Videor: I come unseen.* For this reason, their activities in wartime remain almost unknown although the price paid by them was extremely high.

During the six years of war from 1939 to 1945, submarine losses on all sides amounted to nearly 1,200 vessels which failed to return from patrols. Lost with the German U Boats, more than thirty thousand Submariners failed to reach a home port. These figures represented 80% of U Boats sent out on operations. Japan lost 64%, Italy 57%, Britain 33% (about one third of these being due to enemy mines). The United States losses were proportionately low, 18% This was due, mainly, to the Japanese Navy's poor anti-submarine tactics and equipment.'

U-Boot 1051 was one of the Type VII C. submarines with a displacement of 769 tons. The builder was Germania-Werft at Kiel. Laid down on the 11th of February, 1943 the vessel was completed for service in 1944. It served with the 5th. U-Boot Flotilla until, at the beginning of January, 1945, it became a unit with the 11th Flotilla for its last voyage.

The pressure hull had been strengthened to allow for deeper diving which could take it below the maximum 500 feet depth of British depth charges. The dimensions of this class of boat were 220.25 feet overall with a beam of 20.25 feet and a depth of 15.75 feet. It was, therefore, a sizeable vessel for those days, being propelled by twin screw diesel electric motors which produced 2,800 horsepower on the surface or 750 horse power when submerged. U 1051 was capable of 17 knots on the surface or a maximum of 7½ knots when submerged, both these maximums being fast for wartime submarines.

U 1172, also, was a Type VII C laid down on 7th June, 1943 and completed by 20th April, 1944 at the Danziger Werft Builders. At first, it was attached to the 8th U Boot Flotilla from its commissioning in April 1944 until, like U 1051, it joined the 11th Flotilla at the end of December 1944.

The fuel tanks of the VII C submarines were sufficient to carry 114 tons of fuel oil which gave a range of 6,500 miles at 12 knots or 4 knots submerged with the schnorkel operating. Armaments consisted of five 21 inch torpedo tubes, four forward and one aft, and stowage for fourteen torpedoes, a 3.5 inch gun and one 37 mm anti aircraft and another two 20 mm guns. U 1172 was fitted with a schnorkel which allowed her to run the diesel engines to a depth of about 30 feet and showing above water a mere two feet of this exhaust and air inlet.

Ober Lieutenant Heinrich von Holleben was Commanding Officer for a total complement of forty seven submariners, highly trained and, even at the end of the fifth year of the war, courageous men of high morale. Lt Kuhlmann commanded a crew of forty six men. Both U 1051 and U 1172 sailed together on the 15th January, 1945 after the Christmas break when the new strategy had been finalised. At that time *Manners* was in dry dock at Falmouth having received a dent in her bows from that negligent, gale driven dredger.

The final voyage of U 1051 began in Bergen and took the northerly route around the north of England and it must, therefore, have entered the Irish Sea at the northern end. It reached the southern side of Liverpool Bay where the Motor ship *Vigsnes* was sunk on the 23rd January.

During the three days interval prior to sighting *Manners*, U 1051 must have cruised very slowly in the area to the north and west of Anglesey, using the cover of night-time to charge batteries as a preparation for the voyage back to Bergen or one of the submarine bases in Germany. This meant the hazardous voyage around the north of Scotland. During these three days, Lt. Holleben must have anticipated meeting up with large merchant ships entering or leaving Liverpool. His failure to do so may have prompted him to go for the smaller vessel, thus putting ships like *Manners* at risk.

Royal Naval frigates and destroyers were organised either as escort

(Photo: Sub. Lt. David Gibson, RNVR)

Members of a happy crew sun-it on the Quarterdeck.

or support groups; the Escort group protected ships in convoy while the Support group roamed the seas in search of the enemy. In the first month of 1945, three groups were in the Irish Sea. The 5th Escort Group consisted of the Senior ship, *Aylmer,* commanded by Commander B.W. Taylor; *Tyler* with Lt. C.H. Tonkin in charge; *Bligh* with Lt. Commander J.W. Cooper, RNR; *Keats* commanded by Lt. Commander N.E. Isreal, RNR; *Kempthorne* with Lt. Commander A Brown, RNR. This vessel had served in the Atlantic, the Italian invasions, D. Day landings, and Russian Convoys before voyaging through the Irish Sea. After escorting the damaged *Manners* to Barrow in Furness, she entered Glasgow docks, where she was seriously sabotaged, never serving again with the Group. *Bickerton* with Lt. E.M. Thorpe had been lost in the August of the previous year while operating with a Russian Convoy.

The 4th Escort Group consisted of *Bentinck*, the Senior ship had been in the charge of Commander E.H. Chavasse – later the Reverend Evelyn Chavasse, DSO, DSC, OBE; but Commander R Garwood, RN had assumed command towards the end of 1944. *Calder* commanded by Lt. Commander E Playne, RNVR; *Bazely* Lt. Commander J.V. Brock, RCNVR; *Drury*, Lt. Commander N.J. Parker and *Pasely* Lt. P.G. Mitchell and *Byard* Lt. Commander K Ferris, RNVR.

The 21st Escort Group with the Senior Officer, Lt. Commander R. Hart in *Conn* was composed of six Captain Class frigates, Lt. K.C.L. Southcombe in *Byron*; *Redmill*, later torpedoed in Donegal Bay with the loss of 27 crew; *Rupert* Lt. P.C.S. Black; *Deane* Lt. V.A. Hickson and *Fitzroy*, Lt. Commander P.J. Miller, RNVR.

On 21st January, 1945 a small convoy from the Thames to Bristol was attacked four miles to the south west of Lands End. U-Boat 1199, commanded by Lt. Stollmann managed to torpedo an American ship in this convoy, the *George Hawley* of 7,176 tons. Although severely damaged, the ship was taken in tow by the tug *Allegiance* which managed to get her into Falmouth Harbour. U 1199 was attacked by HMS *Icarus* and *Mignonette* and destroyed. The corvette, *Mignonette,* was one of the escorting vessels and contact with U 1199 was obtained fifteen minutes after the torpedoing. The U Boat was damaged in the first attack and sought refuge on the bottom close to the Wolf Rock. At 1540. the destroyer *Icarus* from the 14th Escort Group carried out one hedgehog and two depth charge attacks after which wood, oil and large air bubbles were observed coming to the surface. One survivor was picked up. He said that he was in the control room of the enemy vessel, U 1199 which was hit and began filling with water. He had escaped by opening the hatch and coming to the surface in an air bubble, the only one to do so.

On that same day, a small Norwegian coaster of 1,152 tons, the *Galatea*, registered in Bergen, was proceeding in ballast independently to Liverpool from Barry with a crew of eighteen, plus three DEMS gunners. This vessel was attacked and sunk with only one survivor who was picked up next day by HMS *Tyler*. The attack was carried out either by Lt. Stölker commanding U-Boat 825. or Lt Kuhlmann in U-Boat 1172. The position of this sinking was to the S.W. of Bardsey Island, 52° 40N 05° 23W., more or less in the middle of the Channel. U 825 reported three detonations and one ship probably sunk. This submarine was one of the few to return to Germany undamaged from these operations in the Irish Sea.

After hostilities ended, U 825 was among the hundred or so vessels which surrendered to the Allies in May and June, 1945 before being taken by the British Operation Deadlight to deep water in the Atlantic and sunk. At that time, more than three hundred U Boats had been either scuttled by crews in their home ports or sunk at sea.

An inward bound convoy, number HX 332, was attacked at 1213. on 27th January, one day after our own attack to the north This convoy was being escorted on the last part of its voyage from Halifax by four Escorts of the Canadian C7. Escort group. These were HMCSs *Lanark, Hawkesbury, Copper Cliff* and *Owen Sound*. Lt. Commander R. Hart, DSC RN, Senior Officer of the 21st Escort Group, after supporting a convoy to Milford Haven returned to 51° 48'N 07° 13'W to rendezvous with HX 332. At 0500, at the southern entrance to St. George's Channel, the convoy reformed into two columns and the

Bristol Channel section, escorted by one frigate detached.

Lt. Stölker in U. 825 managed to torpedo two ships in the convoy, the merchant vessel *Solör* of 8,262 tons and the *Ruben Dario* of 7,198 tons. Torpedoes struck these two ships within two and a half minutes of each other. *Ruben Dario* was struck in Number two hold but managed to reach Liverpool under her own power. *Solör* was taken in tow by tugs bound for Milford Haven. She was holed in the engine room and liable to sink at any moment, The *Solör* was beached in Oxwich Bay to the west of Swansea but became a total loss.

After this attack, the 5th Escort Group – which had come south after our own torpedoing and the sinking of U 1051 – and the 21st Escort Group, persisted in a two day search and attack until success was achieved by HMS *Keats* commanded by Lt. Commander N.F. Isreal and ably assisted by HMS *Tyler* and *Bligh*. There was little doubt that a hedgehog attack had achieved the sinking of U 1127 commanded by Lt. Kuhlmann and manned by a crew of forty six. There were no survivors and the sea conditions made it too difficult to pick up wreckage of rubber dinghies and other material sighted. However, two dinghies were washed ashore in Anglesey several days later and these were sent to the Admiralty for identification.

As the time approached for departing from Falmouth for our lone voyage through the Irish Sea to Liverpool, there were, therefore, at least four U Boats operating along our route to Liverpool and a further one or two in the northern section of the Sea. Almost certainly acting in unison, U 1051, commanded by Lt. Cmd. V. Holleben seemed to cover the area around Anglesey, U 1172 with Lt. Kuhlmann in charge was just to the north of Tuskar Rock Lighthouse and Lt. Stölker in U 825 was between the two and U 1199 in the area of Lands End. Probably working as a team but not in contact with each other, the Officers and Men of these U Boats must have shown extraordinary courage merely to get into those positions. Minefields existed on either side of the Irish Sea and at either end of it and, in the both horizontally and vertically confined waters, chances for escape, once detected by our ships, must have been very limited.

It could be that entrance to the relatively confined and well defended area of the Irish Sea had been achieved by submerging beneath an inward bound ship and following it while submerged and without schnorkels operating. In this case, however, maximum speed was no more than a mere seven knots, this being achieved only with a severe drain on the batteries.

Unbeknown to us at anchor in Falmouth Harbour on the 21st January, either this submarine or U 825, commanded by Lt. Stölker sank two further ships towards the southern end of the Irish Sea, while in the north and two days later, on the 23rd of the month, U 1051, commanded by Lt. Commander Heinrick von Holleben, sank *Vigsnes*, a small Norwegian vessel of 1,599 tons which was travelling independently after detaching from convoy MH1 from Cardiff to the Mersey. The entire crew of twenty five managed to land themselves safely in their own boats. This sinking took place at 53° 33'N 04° 17'W, a mere ten miles to the NE of the Skerries Rock, just inside Liverpool Bay.

It was this series of sinkings, together with those taking place throughout the length of the English Channel which decided the Commander in Chief Western Approaches, Admiral Sir Max Horton, to petition the Admiralty to re-route all troop convoys by way of the North Channel and to the west of Ireland. The Admiralty concurred for the time in which the U. Boat threat in the Irish Sea persisted

Up to the time of her sailing from Falmouth, none of the submarines operating along the expected courses of *Manners* had been detected and, more surprisingly, their possible positions remained un-notified to us, about to pass through the area. We remained, therefore, oblivious of dangers strung out along our lone route to Liverpool.

CHAPTER FOUR

Rendezvous
with U-Boat 1051

Manners sailed from Falmouth at 1600 hrs on the 25th January, 1945. The end of the German war was already within sight, our Allied armies well on the way through Europe to the heart of German territory. Russia formed the second front and the evil world of Hitler was being squeezed relentlessly towards our final victory, only four months away. As a result, our watchkeeping activities may well have been a little more relaxed than normal, especially in view of the fact that, without being warned of the battle already in progress throughout the length and breadth of the Irish Sea, we could consider it a reasonably safe area in which to navigate. Courses were set in order to proceed along the swept channels and Zig-zag diagram number eight was in operation from the start of the voyage.

The 'Foxers' were streamed before increasing speed to eighteen knots for the voyage to Liverpool. However, at 1945 hrs the Asdic set was closed down because, at eighteen knots, it became difficult to hear any echo above the inevitable water noises. Furthermore, Asdic transmissions could be heard underwater for many miles and might attract submarines to come and take a look. It could be, therefore, that high speed rendered the use of Asdics of more use to an enemy than to ourselves.

In the very early morning, we passed abeam of the Tuskar Rock Lighthouse in Ireland, expecting to be in Liverpool within another twelve hours or so. Weather was very fair with a Force 3 wind from the south east, giving us a calm sea and visibility of five miles. Everything helped to ensure a quiet passage through the channel between minefields on both sides of us. At 0615 hrs, we received a signal to investigate a radar contact in position 52° 54' N, 05° 20' W. At that time, our position was some forty miles to the south of this position; it took us two hours fifteen minutes to reach it, having maintained Zig-zab Number Eight and our maximum continuous speed.

On reaching the vicinity of this position, course was altered to 270° in order to pass around the contact. This manoeuvre enabled us to spot two liferafts at 0830. They were both empty but inscribed with the name *Galatea*. They indicated, also, that they belonged to a ship registered in Bergen. We never discovered from where these liferafts might have come. The Flag Officer in Charge at the Milford Haven signal station seemed to suggest that the radar contact had been the merchant ship *Supremity* bound for Glasgow from London

This was hard to reconcile with the name on the two lifeboats. We did not know at that time that the parent ship, *Galatea* had been sunk five days before and some fourteen miles to the south in a position 52°40'N 5°23'W. This sinking had been the result of the torpedo attack carried out by Lt. Kuhlmann's U Boat 1172. It was, of course, the parent ship of the two lifeboats sighted by us.

Manners returned to a northerly course of 011° until 0955 when a further alteration was made to the previous course of 006°. The first alteration of course, to take us round the Skerries Rock Light on the north coast of Anglesey, was made soon afterwards, this being to 031°. The forenoon watch took over at 0800 hrs. The Asdic set was re-activated in this watch in order to check the Foxers by listening to them. One of these was intermittent as though one of the metal bars had worn through. This was half expected in so far as they were then operating beyond their recommended life. However, it was thought more reasonable to leave them as they were than to stop the ship in order to recover and change them. Furthermore, in ignorance of the several sinkings in the previous four days, it was a logical assumption that, in those waters, U Boats would attack only when a major target presented.

The Watch was not too concerned as we were inside the mine-fields. It would be very risky for a German U Boat to try and penetrate these and to do so would involved great courage and some hazard on the part of a German Commanding Officer. What we did not know was that five U boats were operating with success within the Irish Sea and that three of these were in St. George's Channel, through which Manners must pass.

At 1042 hrs precisely, an explosion occurred. Some ten seconds after it, there were further heavy explosions some distance astern of us. Almost certainly, these were our own anti-Gnat depth charge blown over the side. This charge was always set to fifty feet in case of need and when it exploded several others, blown over the side with it, were countermined.

These explosions took place during the morning Stand Easy. We rushed to Action Stations, soon realising that we had suffered a Gnat torpedo strike in the stern, just below the NAAFI Canteen in which William Ribchester, our NAAFI Manager, was dispensing the usual edibles and cigarettes. The explosion was not a major one, but strong enough to separate my cup from its saucer and break it against the deck head.

Our Commanding Officer, Lieutenant Jermain, RN asked me to leave the bridge and obtain a full report from the First Lieutenant. I found him working in the NAAFI Canteen – which was over the position of the port side propeller. Both propellers were out of action and the ship was slowing down quickly. Damage Control reported to the Bridge that, so far as the hull was concerned, damage was not too serious, there were five or six casualties of which the worst was two broken legs. Some fifty members of the Damage Control team were closed up in the area of damage, shoring bulkheads, attending to the wounded and clearing the mess.

William Ribchester, was among the injured. The report of Lieutenant Carter included these details but also that the casualties were not high but that the stern was buckled and the quarter deck given a camber. One of our smoke cannisters had been thrown for-

3" Gunnery Practice. Lt. D. Jermain middle left. Lt. D.W. Collins next to him, black and no hat.

(Photo: A. Russell Stewart)

ward to cause smoke in the engine room. It must have dropped through the engine room skylight in order to manage this. Otherwise, the ship returned to the upright position but with a slight list until this was corrected by Engine Room Staff pumping fuel oil from the port side tanks to the starboard. The remainder of the hull, at that time, appeared to be watertight.

Later, I heard that one of our Quartermasters, Able Seaman Ronald Bloomfield had a providential escape in spite of receiving head injuries and a crushed back. He managed to reach the upper deck by way of a damaged step ladder. He tried several times to stand up but his legs were like rubber and unable to support him. He heard someone call for help, so shouted out his name and a promise to try and get help. He was eventually carried up to 'X' Gun deck and then amidships. Immediately after arriving in that safer area, the second explosion occurred.

Jack Butcher, Stoker 1st Class did not survive. He volunteered to enter the after flat below the mess deck. He took with him a flood light to search for survivors and was last seen in three or four feet of water, just before the second explosion and prior to the stern breaking off and sinking.

Leading Telegraphist Russell Stewart may well owe his life to a break with his usual custom of visiting the Canteen late in opening time, hopping down early in order to be in the front of the queue. He left the Canteen, therefore, at 10.35, complete with his 'Nutty' and cigarettes, together with a supply of these items for those on watch in the W/T Office. He returned along the upper deck, taking the ladder to the door of his Office. There, he stood chatting to Telegraphist Phillip Barnley, noticing the Hospital ship in sight ahead of us.

Both these Telegraphists were looking towards our stern when the depth charge rails appeared to rise above 'Y' Gun deck, disintegrating as they flew into the air. *"They seemed to break into a thousand pieces before our eyes,"* said Telegraphist Russell Stewart. He assumed that a depth charge had exploded, realising immediately how providential had been his early visit to the Canteen; another two

or three minutes would have meant his presence among those taking the full brunt of the first explosion. He ducked into the W/T
Office, remaining there until the second explosion caused him to
look out of the door. At his feet, lying dead on the deck was his
friend and fellow Telegraphist Phillip Harry Barnley. He must have
been struck by descending debris. His immediate thought was,
"What a sad ending to a happy ship."

As I reached the bridge to deliver the First Lieutenant's report, the
second torpedo hit us at a spot about twenty or thirty feet from the
stern. It was a heavy explosion intended, obviously, for the engine
room. We were saved from this, however, because – even ten minutes after the first torpedo – the ship was still making way. In the
time it took for the torpedo to travel three thousand yards, the ship
had moved ninety feet.

With shock, we knew immediately that half our complement had
gone to the bottom with the wreck of our stern. Lieutenant (E)
Riches, RNR had been in charge of the Damage Control team, num-
bering about fifty people, the First Lieutenant had been assisting him.
Lieutenant Collins – who had received in Falmouth a letter from his
wife informing him that they had a new son – had been inspecting
damage to ammunition and helping the injured, and the youngest
member of the Wardroom, Sub Lieutenant George Glynn was secur-
ing depth charges in the stern racks. He was blown upwards for
about sixty feet before descending and hitting our 'X' Gun deck.

At the same time at which I had seen George above us, I saw ten
feet of heavy chain, with links about five inches long, soaring over
our heads, almost certainly going to hit the bridge. Instead, however, it wrapped itself around the mast some twenty feet above us.
There were fifty seven casualties of whom only fourteen were
injured and a further one, Joseph Stephenson, was slightly injured.

That figure of fifty seven meant that more than half the entire crew
had been lost to us. The number of dead might have been slightly
increased had it not been for the Hospital Ship *Atlantis* which was
the only vessel within sight, some miles ahead of us. Because we

were unable to raise her by signal lamp, our Commanding Officer ordered a shot to be placed in front of her bows. This was effective and she sent a boat to us in order to begin the transfer of the severely wounded. *Atlantis* was travelling empty to Liverpool but she had on board her usual complement of doctors and nurses and facilities for blood transfusions

The pressure on our own Surgeon and Sick Bay Staff was, thereby, alleviated. Surgeon Lt. Michael Connell and Sick Berth Attendant, J. Huskie, aided by Able Seaman Spenser, continued to save lives and assist the injured. One of those saved by this medical team was Able Seaman Ronald Bloomfield who remembers being laid, very carefully, on the upper deck of MTB 778 next to the Gunnery Officer, Lt. Collins.

Three Motor Torpedo boats were sent out from their anchorage in Holyhead. HMMTBs 778. and 767 came alongside at 1240 hrs and complimented the work of transferring our seriously wounded to HS 'Atlantis,' while M.B 762 stood by. About three weeks later, on the 14th February, 1945, this MTB Squadron experienced a severe mauling at the raid on Ostend and MTB 765, together with ten others, was sunk by explosions and fire.

Surgeon Lieutenant Connell fought hard to save the life of the Gunnery Officer, before laying him on a stretcher on the upper deck of MTB 778 beside Able Seaman Bloomfield for the short trip to *Atlantis*. He had been hit on the shoulder by a descending depth charge. This had collapsed his entire right side and he died on the way over to the Hospital Ship. Two others, Able Seaman Stanley Bernard Pym and Chief Petty Officer (E) Thomas Norris died on that same trip to the Hospital Ship. Two further deaths occurred after reaching the medical wards on *Atlantis*, Able Seaman Herbert Angold and Able Seaman Fred Hardy.

J. Huskie, our Sick Berth Attendant, further distinguished himself after the last of the wounded had received his care. He was seen recovering the dead from positions of extreme danger to himself. One of the depth charge racks was blown into a position jutting out some ten feet or more over the water. On the end of this rack was a badly mutilated body which SBA Huskie recovered before it could be lost in the sea. He must have suffered great anguish of mind as a result of his efforts for our sick and dead.

The second explosion had sheered off sixty feet of our two hundred and eighty feet length: it had done this so neatly that the break might have been achieved with a saw. The break was just on the outside of a watertight bulkhead. The remaining three fifths of the ship were without leak, the main engines and generators were in order, the radar was functioning normally. The Asdic set alone was without power. *Manners* however, could not move, both propellers having gone to the bottom.

Petty Officer W.R. Foster was a brave man! At a time when he did not know what was going to happen to the ship, he descended to the small cubby hole in which was the oscillator shaft and the motor for raising and lowering the oscillator dome. To gain access to this spot, he had opened two watertight hatches, the bottom one of which was but eighteen inches across. His electrical knowledge restored power to the Asdic set and he returned to the bridge. He operated the set with Able Seaman B. Beeby SD and managed to obtain an echo from a submarine lying on the bottom of the sea. It was at a little over maximum range but he held onto this echo for three hours, almost certainly causing the submarine to remain on the sea bed without the chance to fire the third torpedo.

It could be that the first torpedo was fired because the U 1051 assumed us to be on an attacking course. This could have been the reason for attacking a minor target in confined waters. On our new course of 031° the submarine was directly ahead of us, having noticed, no doubt, our alteration to that new course – and we were approaching at eighteen knots!

During our long hours of waiting for someone to tow us to port, the ship was restored to some semblance of order, watches were reorganised and those who were dead on board were laid out by our Sick Bay Staff. I checked the mess deck adjacent to the torpedo damage, meeting a Petty Officer coming up the stairway after doing just that. However, I went down to find one of the watertight doors open. This door had connected with the next compartment but now it opened onto nothing but water. It was a mere ten inches or so above the sea. I closed it, therefore, making sure that all six clips surrounding it were firmly in place. I returned to the deck where I mentioned to the P.O. that he had forgotten one of the doors. He was so amazed that, together, we returned below. Both of us were rather shattered to find the door swinging on its hinges. We closed it again, this time using a bar slipped over each clip which was then pulled down with our combined weights. Ten minutes later, that door was open again! No one had been into that compartment, most being rather fearful of entering in view of the proximity of torpedo damage and one or two broken depth charges lashed to stanchions above. Both the P.O. and I remained totally convinced that the door could not have opened itself. But how?

The heavy chain which had been blown from the Quarter deck to entangle itself in the crosstree and wireless aerials had to be got down before the radio could call for help. All the radio fuses had to be withdrawn to make it safe for someone to climb aloft and untangle the chain before lowering it to the deck. After doing this, he looked downwards to notice, in the funnel, between the two hot exhausts, a depth charge! These weigh four hundred and fifty pounds and this one must have been blown upwards by the explosion in order for it to drop into the funnel.

It was about six feet down, having dented both exhausts all the way down. The pistol, containing the detonator was downwards, though the primer could be withdrawn first from the top. It was the normal, safe practice, however, for the detonator to be withdrawn first as it was the delicate item. It was so delicate that it could explode if dropped for two feet, this one must have dropped a hundred feet! In the present case, it might have been more dangerous to use force with which to turn the depth charge over as it was split open and jammed in that position.

Depth charges were in the care of the Anti-submarine Officer – myself! On looking for the non-spark spanners with which to withdraw the detonator, I found that all of them had gone down with the stern part of the ship. I did not tell the Engine Room Artificer, in whose province was the funnel, how dangerous it was to hit the nut round with a hammer and chisel: at one time, he held the chisel and I tapped it and he was a bit churlish when I did not hit it very hard! But we got it out, withdrawing the pistol. This I carried to the top of the funnel and threw it as hard as I could into the sea. From that moment, things were safe. A block and tackle hauled the charge out and it was lashed on deck with the assistance of Joseph Jones, one of the Asdic team.

As I climbed out of the funnel, I could not help but notice a number of the crew standing on the very tip of the bow and wondering why; until, some time later, I realised that the rumour of 'depth charge in the funnel' must have flown round the ship and the bows were as far away as one could get! I wish I could remember the name of that Engineroom Artificer, even if only to tell him how dangerous we were in using undue force on a primed and detonated amatol charge. His hand was badly gashed during our exploit!

At the end of two hours of waiting, our sister ships, HMS *Calder*, commanded by Lt. Commander E Playne, RNVR.; *Bentinck* by Commander R. Garwood RN and *Aylmer* Commander B.W. Taylor, RN reached us. We gave the range and bearing of the submarine and these ships ran over the spot but without being able to obtain a contact. We requested *Calder* to range on us with radar, while we passed by light, the range and bearing of our submarine echo. When the two coincided, *Calder* fired a pattern of Hedgehog depth charges. This type of charge is fired ahead of the ship in a pattern of eight. One of them made a direct hit on the conning tower of U 1051 which was forced, thereby, to surface. No effort to abandon the submarine was apparent so all three ships engaged with 3" gunfire before *Aylmer*, taking no chances, turned and rammed at full speed, hitting the submarine just ahead of its conning tower. It remained impaled on

Aylmer's bows for long enough for three other frigates, *Calder*, *Bentinck* and *Bligh* to close in to water hose range! Certainly, one ship used this type of weapon to stop U Boat survivors – who had appeared on deck – getting to the gun. The U Boat 1051 sank, however, and no Submariners survived. The position of the sinking was 53° 39'N 5° 21'W! *Manners* was credited with a major share in this victory, even though lying, badly damaged, some miles to the south

On her run in to ram, *Aylmer* had noticed a motif painted on the conning tower. This consisted of a pink shield bearing the figure '7.' Across the '7' was a bar in the form of a fish, this being a very good description of the wappen painted on U 1051. It was only in 1992 that the importance of this identification mark was fully appreciated and an error of maritime history was corrected. Prior to that year, it had been assumed that Lt. Kuhlmann's U 1172 was responsible for our loss, together with that of *Vigsnes* three days before. U 1051 was thought to have been responsible for the loss of *Galatea* one hundred miles to the south on the 21st January. Because the wappen on U 1051 was seen by *Aylmer* this historical error was rectified. Both submarines, however, were sunk without survivors; U 1051 a few hours after our torpedoing and some miles to the north of us by *Aylmer*, *Calder*, *Bentinck* and *Bligh* and ourselves, even though we lay immobile two miles away from the final action.

The forward lower compartment of *Aylmer* was flooded. Her damage control managed to shore up the bulkhead and course was altered for Holyhead, the nearest port. *Aylmer* began the voyage stern first but finished it under her own power. She was escorted by two frigates, *Bligh* and *Tyler*. both of which were to share, with *Keats*, in the sinking of U 1172 on the 27th January, 1945, the day after our own loss.

Eventually, at 1400 hrs the tug, PC 74, reached us and began the tow to Barrow in Furness. In attendance and escorting us were HMS *Grindall* and HMS *Kempthorne*. The position in which the stern of *Manners* sank with so many of our crew members is given in the War Diary, Home Command, for 26th January, 1945 as 280° 21 miles from the Skerries Rocks Lighthouse. This position is within a matter of a mile or two of the course taken by Sealink ferries crossing from Dun Laoghaire to Holyhead. I have sometimes requested a visit to the bridge when making that ferry crossing, thus recalling the burial there of so many of my wartime Shipmates.

A member of the crew of HMS *Bligh*, which passed close to Manners in order to offer assistance, remarked that *"Manners looks a sorry sight."* PC 74 began the tow to Barrow in Furness in the hopes that Vickers Naval Yard could restore us to a whole ship. The tow, however, was slow and at about 0100 hrs on 27th January one of our escorting destroyers came in very close to the tow-line and dropped a pattern of charges on a possible submarine echo. This parted the tow-line and created havoc on the nerves of our crew resting up after their ordeal. I was on watch at the time, sensing the parting of the tow-line before it became apparent. To retie the knot meant calling out some of the off-watch men who laboured long and hard to heave the new line aboard and secure it.

Manners reached the quayside in the outer harbour at Barrow in Furness about twenty five hours after disaster had struck. Two Wren Officers came into the Wardroom in order to deliver secret mail, one saying over the coffee, *"I have seen many Captain Class Frigates but never one as short as this."* I think it was Lieutenant Frank Collett, now serving in place of the First Lieutenant, who replied, *"Ah, that's in order to make it more difficult to be hit by torpedo!"*

Our crew was granted seven days 'Survivors' Leave' but prior to catching our trains, it became known that our ship had been considered damaged beyond economic repair and would be used as spare parts for other frigates. This meant the break up of what had been a very happy and contented crew. We could not help recalling to each other moments of humour and excitement offered by those no longer with us: the time in a Spelling Bee, for instance, when the Engineer, God rest his soul, was invited to spell 'auspice.' He appeared to think hard before starting, *"H – O – R – S....."* when he was stopped by the Questionmaster who butted in, saying, *"Not that sort, try 'auspicious' instead."* Or the time when George – blown up before our eyes – volunteered to organise the guest list of Wrens for a Wardroom film show (which was 'John Halifax Gentleman'). He managed to find no less than ten charming Wrens, all with the name, Joan. What with the irony of the film which demanded our warning thoughts to be voiced aloud to the heroine of the film, and the confusion over names, the party became hilarious.

It has always occasioned me great comfort to know that of all the Catholics who died on the 26th January, 1945, every single one had received the Sacraments of Confession and Communion on the day before, during our visit to Canon Fanning's Church in Falmouth.

I remained with *Manners* for several weeks, and when my turn arrived for a change, most of the others had been re-appointed to other ships. I was to join HMS *Begum* under the command of Captain Howe, RN She had been an American cargo ship before conversion to a Royal Navy Light Aircraft Carrier. The ship was due to go to the Pacific and Japanese area of the War. The first voyage was to be to the Admiralty Isles in the Bismarck Archipelago with a load of large bombs and aircraft to be unloaded in Manus Isle before proceeding south again to Sydney in New South Wales.

Manners was de-commissioned and returned to the custody of the American Navy on 8th November, 1945. She was struck from the Navy Register on 19th December – exactly two years after the date of her commissioning in Boston. She was then sold on 3rd December, 1946 to the Athens Piraeus Electricity Company Limited in Greece for scrapping. She arrived there on 7th January, 1947, almost exactly three years after her maiden voyage.

CHAPTER FIVE

The Sinking of U-Boat 1051

The Fifth Escort Group had consisted of *Bickerton*, *Aylmer*, *Bligh*, *Goodson*, *Keats* and *Kempthorne*. After serving in the Atlantic, Italy, D.Day and Russian Convoys, the Group was left with *Aylmer*, *Bligh*, and *Keats*. *Bickerton* had been lost in a Russian Convoy and *Goodson* was sunk on D. Day. Kempthorne was seriously sabotaged in Glasgow and never joined the group again. The three ships surviving in the Group operated independently or with ships of other groups, and they played a role in meeting convoys or with the support groups.

The Ordnance Artificer on Bligh, Tom Kennie, gave his version of the attack and ramming of U 1051:

> "The news came to us that *Manners* had been torpedoed at 1052 on the morning of 26th January, 1945. *Bligh* and *Aylmer* got a contact on the U Boat at about 1400 that afternoon and a creeper attack was mounted, together with *Bentinck* and *Calder*. On contact being achieved *Bligh* and *Aylmer* dropped depth charges. *Calder* followed this attack with Hedgehogs. This attack succeeded in obtaining one hit which brought the U Boat to the surface between *Bligh* and *Bentinck*. at about 1600 in the afternoon. I was the Ordnance Artificer and everyone opened fire with 3" guns but the shells from *Bligh* were ricocheting and hitting *Bentinck*. *Aylmer*, being the senior ship, told us to hold fire and she would do what was required. *Aylmer* went full ahead and hit the U Boat amidships. The U Boat remained firmly embedded in the *Aylmer*'s bows for

some minutes during which time we were only about 30-50 yards away from the encounter. The *Aylmer* was holed pretty badly but able to make way for Holyhead and then, I understood, to Liverpool. We were within 50 yards of the *Aylmer* and we all feared that the sinking submarine was going to take *Aylmer* with it.

"When the U boat surfaced it was between *Bligh* and *Bentinck*. *Aylmer* was doing a U turn and told us, as she was the senior ship, to cease fire and she would take charge. The U boat was surfaced and turning slowly to port and *Aylmer* came between *Bligh* and *Bentinck* and rammed this U Boat amidships. At one time, I assumed that figures walking in the smoke and steam were German submariners who had managed to escape through one of the hatches. It could be that, with the bow of *Aylmer* very low in the water, these figures were our own seamen."

Mr. Grills was the port lookout on the bridge of *Aylmer* throughout the action. He told me that they had heard a very heavy explosion at 1040 as they came up the Irish Sea. This must have been the countermining of several of our own depth charges, blown overboard by the first Gnat strike and exploding together astern of us.

"We were then about fifty miles to the south of *Manners*. Only one explosion was heard and it was something of a surprise to us to learn that there were two torpedoes and a third explosion caused by several depth charges being blown over the stern and then countermined by the anti-Gnat depth charge, always primed, detonated and set ready for dropping if needed.

"We passed to starboard of *Manners* at about 1300hrs or two and a half hours after the sound of that explosion. We saw *Manners* immobile in the water and in a very sorry state. We joined the attack already taking place against the submarine which was then a few miles to the north of *Manners*. Assisting in this hunt and attack were *Aylmer*, *Calder* and *Bligh* and

Bentinck. A creep attack eventually paid off and contact was
made with the U 1051. Calder carried out a Hedgehog attack
and scored one hit which brought the submarine to the surface.
We all opened fire with our 3" guns and Oerlikons and I saw
some of the shells ricocheting off the water in a cloud of steam.
Some of these shells were hitting *Bentinck*. As a result, a cease
fire was ordered by *Aylme*r which then turned sharply to fin-
ish the job. We rammed the submarine, just ahead of the conning tower at eighteen knots, *Aylmer* coming in at a 45° angle.

"We hit with such force that the ship heeled right over and
everyone was flung off their feet, many suffering blackened
eyes or bruises. The submarine appeared to be on fire and
impaled into our bows so firmly that our bows went down
almost to water level. The stern rose out of the water so much
that we probably could not go astern as the propellers were
half out of the water.

"The submarine remained in that position for about five
minutes; smoke and steam was thick. It may have been this
smoke which caused the *Bligh* on our starboard side to assume
that our crew members walking on our much lowered fo'castle were survivors who had managed to get out of the conning
tower. This is not so, however, as no one could have opened
the conning tower hatch as damage was bad. They were probably much knocked about and confused by what was going on
in the submarine itself: water entering under pressure through
damage to the hull; perhaps gas from the batteries and the confusion resulting from no lighting; noise, the severe list and
damage from the Hedgehog attack.

"After those few minutes of remaining locked in our bows,
the submarine began to sink by the stern and we feared it
might take us with it. However, it broke free and eventually
went down with the bows vertical in the air. There was an
immense cheer from the crews of all four ships then present at
very short range. Everyone, however, must have felt awesome

concern for those suffering from terrifying events inside that helpless wreck.

"Damage to *Aylmer* was severe, our bows smashed as far back as the Asdic dome, about forty feet from the stem. There was not a single usable cup left in the ship, all being smashed by the jolt and sudden list to port. Damage control teams shored up various bulkheads and we were taken in tow for a stern-first voyage of thirty fives miles to Holyhead. However, in Holyhead there was no dry dock large enough to take our two hundred and ninety feet. We put to sea again, bound for Liverpool, ninety miles to the east. This voyage was made under our own steam."

"This submarine attack was the second time in the Irish Sea that we had assisted another ship which had suffered heavy casualties. HMS *Whittaker*, commanded by Lt. G.D.W. Edwards, RN, had been so severely damaged by torpedo, two months before, that not a single Officer survived and there were ninety two casualties in a total complement of about one hundred. We escorted the wreck into Belfast where the dock-yard workers refused to extricate the very badly mutilated bodies inside the bridge area. Our crew, therefore, undertook this gruesome task and our Commanding Officer saw to it that every man had extra rum tots. The vessel was so badly damaged that she was scrapped at Larne eighteen months later."

Dick Roberts, the starboard lookout on *Aylmer*, recounted how his ship had made several runs and attacks on a submarine contact, at least one other ship making similar attacks between 1300 and 1600 on the 26th January, 1945. No diesel oil nor wreckage came to the surface. Towards the end of the afternoon, some four or five ships were circling around the contact. Dick continued:

"The Group Captain on our ship ordered a depth charge attack and then a hedgehog attack at 1609 hours. *Calder* went in to fire the hedgehog pattern, after which there was one explosion which brought the sub to the surface. Everyone start-

The hurricane of November 1944.

(Photo: Sub. Lt. David Gibson, RNVR)

ing firing guns.

"Eventually, *Aylmer* decided to ram and we were told to hold on tight to anything we could lay our hands on as there was going to be a crash. As soon as we hit the sub, we had a very severe shaking. The conning tower was on fire and badly damaged and, as the sub. went down, I saw three or four trying to get out but after she disappeared there was no trace of any survivor. Our Captain went in to ram because the crew of the sub. were still aboard, increasing the danger of torpedoes being fired at us and the other ships close by. The crash damaged us pretty badly and we sailed for Holyhead which was about thirty miles away. As the dock was not big enough for us, we sailed again for Gladstone Dock in Liverpool for a refit."

There are two reports in the sixth volume of the wartime Monthly Anti Submarine Report, 1945 Lt. Commander E. Playne, RNVR, Commanding Officer of HMS *Calder*, states that at 1230:-

"I was on the starboard beam of *Bentinck* when we approached *Manners*.

At 1300 turned to port for a contact 348° 1,000 yards.

1312 Could not obtain an echo although I passed through the position given by *Bentinck*. *Bentinck* was in contact from the southward, suggesting that the U- Boat was stern on to me.

1319 *Bentinck* dropped D/C pattern.

1328 I passed through the position of the pattern from the eastward without gaining contact. 1400. *Bentinck* attacked with D/C.

At 1402 I gained contact for the first time: 253°-1,700 yards.

1407 H/H (Hedgehog attack). No explosions. Contact held down the port side and H.E. (Hydrophone effects) reported.

1417 Turned back to 100° and then to 055° to investigate last position.

1440 E.G. 5. in *Aylmer* was in contact with the submarine. Told him that it was the same one as *Bentinck's*.

1507   Altered course to 090° and then to North to close *Aylmer* who was in contact.

1519   Gained contact: 004° – 2,700 yards.

1525   D/C attack. Set 'F' to explode on the bottom. Target stopped. Contact held right in. *Aylmer* followed with an E/S (Echo sounding) run. The ASCOs were completely satisfied that this was a U-boat. It was only by luck and the good weather that we were able to steer accurately over the target slow enough for a single stylus E/S to show a mark. The importance of the early fitting of four stylus E/S cannot in my opinion be over-estimated.

1550   When the target bore 008°-1,200 yards, I turned to starboard and made Hangover Two by visual light.

1554   The target appeared to be coming towards me and going right towards *Aylmer* who was to the eastward in the perfect position. I asked him to rev up with the idea that the U Boat would turn away from him and present me with a beam-on target and also in the hope that the noise from *Aylmer* would prevent the U Boat hearing my relatively silent approach at eight knots. I overlooked the fact that, by speeding up, *Aylmer* was risking a Gnat but he nobly complied and the result was at 1600. a hit with H/H. Explosion sounded like two bombs hitting not quite simultaneously. 1603. U Boat surfaced, bows on, just as I was turning to port with the result that *Calder* was beam on. I ordered full ahead, Port 30° and was clear very quickly while all guns opened fire. But 'A' Gun got in only one round and 'B' Gun none as the bearing was too far aft until I had to order 'Cease Fire' as *Aylmer* went in to ram."

Commander Playne continues his report with a few observations:
     "As the U Boat was end-on when surfacing, my view of the U Boat was very restricted but she was definitely down by the stern when surfaced. She had no net cutter or gun forward. There was a cutaway portion abaft the bridge with bandstand

rails but these and the bridge appeared to be damaged. This suggests that one bomb hit the bridge and another the hull and accounts for the double explosion. There was no evidence of streamling to suggest a fast U-Boat. This agrees with the plotted speed of 2½ knots. There was no visible sign of a Schnorkel. One of my Officers reports that the forward escape hatch was opened before she sank but no one got out. Quite a lot of damage was done to the conning tower by gun fire but I could see no evidence of penetration of her hull by 3" projectiles."

The Commanding Officer of Aylmer also gave a report of the action:-

> "In brief, it is the story of a familiar bottom contact whose characteristics did not exactly tally with previous experience. More than once it appeared that we were dealing with a non sub but the conviction grew in *Aylmer* that at least we were on to a possible U Boat. For this conviction, I must commend my Group A/S officer Lieutenant N.L.B. Schuster, Royal Navy whose diagnosis proved so right. *Bentinck*, who was joined at 1415, had stated that he had lost contact and instructed me to search to the westward while he proceeded southward.

At 1430   *Aylmer* obtained an A/S contact which I was informed by *Calder* was probably *Bentinck*'s old one.

At 1509   *Aylmer* dropped a D/C pattern 'E', *Calder* following with one on the bottom at 1520.

At 1530   the Group A/S Officer who was on the Asdic phones reported HE of a torpedo approaching the port side. The helm was put hard over and a single charge dropped which may well have misled the U Boat into thinking that he had bagged another victim.

At 1545   *Calder* obtained an echo sounding trace at 75 feet – this so clinched the matter that both ships simultaneously stated their intention of carrying out a Hedgehog attack – the honour was naturally given to *Calder*.

Convoy to Liverpool, mid Atlantic, Christmas Day, 1944.

(Photo: Sub. Lt. David Gibson, RNVR)

At 1559   *Calder* attacked and the fatal explosion was seen in *Aylmer*
who by this time had stemmed the target at a range of
1,200 yards. About three minutes after the attack the bows
of the U Boat appeared at an angle of about 20° up, quickly followed by the whole U Boat which regained considerable buoyancy, the casing top being 6 feet out of the water.
It could be seen that the conning tower had been damaged
but not to a very marked degree.

There appeared to be no attempt by any of the U Boat crew
to abandon ship by any of the hatches and I considered the
possibility of the U Boat emulating some of her predeces-
sors and firing torpedoes – she had already shown an
unpleasantly offensive spirit in firing a torpedo from deep
at 1530. The U Boat was then almost fully surfaced point-
ing straight at *Calder* at a range of about 1,200 yards, and
with slight headway on. *Aylmer* was well placed on its
port beam at a range of about 1,000 yards.

Gunfire was opened by both ships – of the 20 rounds of 3"
fired by *Aylmer* at least four were direct hits on the conning tower, one certainly penetrating before bursting; innu-
merable oerlikon hits were registered.

At 1605   *Aylmer* rammed the U Boat midway between the conning
tower and bows on the port side, cutting through the main
ballast and into the hull. The U Boat immediately started
to fill and, as *Aylmer* backed astern about two minutes
later, sank throwing out large quantities of oil, miscella-
neous wreckage and large bubbles of air.

While the U Boat was wedged in *Aylmer*'s bows one man
was seen to be trying to get out of the hatch just before the
conning tower. The U boat sank too quickly however, and
he was jammed in the hatch. Egress by the Conning Tower
hatch would have been impossible.

The damage to the conning tower was extensive though
there was no sign of the large explosion which might have

been expected from the Hedgehog projectile. The conning
tower casing was riddled with holes from the 3" and the
Oerlikon shells. It is hoped that some photographs taken
by Sub. Lieutenant G.I. Davis, RNVR will prove of value in
identifying the various fittings on the U Boat which was
one of the 500 ton type. Its armament was one 40mm gun
of the bofors type on the fore casing and two single mount-
ing oerlikons on the band stand. The notable feature of the
conning tower was four vertical stanchions about 4 foot 6
inches clear of the the conning tower "beading", two on
either side. The badge was a continental 7, the cross stroke
of which was a fish on a pink shield."

It was the sighting of this German Wappen painted on the port side
of the submarine's conning tower which identified U 1051. On the
starboard side of that conning tower, *Calder* had noticed five small
shields, no doubt recording successes of former voyages. U 1051,
commanded by Ober Lt. Heinrich von Holleben, together with the
other forty six members of the crew lies in position 307° 36.5 miles
from the Skerries Lighthouse on the north coast of Anglesey, or, as
the Western Approaches War Diary states, 23 miles east of Rockabill
in Ireland.

Sometimes there are survivors who manage to escape from a sinking submarine. Their reports indicate the horrors faced by entire
crews who face disaster below the surface. Lt. Gebauer in command
of U 681, for instance, sailed from Kiel on the 7th February, 1945 for
her first patrol. She put into Kristiansand and Bergen where she took
on fuel but because of the growing shortages, especially in Norway,
she received only 100 cubic metres instead of the 130 needed.

From Bergen, course was set to pass between the Shetland Isles
and the Faeroes and, to save oil, kept as close as possible to the
British Isles. Early on 11th March 1945, she reached her operational
area in the south of the Western Approaches. Her Commander took
cross bearings on the Bishop Rock Lighthouse and a disused light on
St. Agnes and from there, in forty fathoms of water, he set a course

of 020° to pass through St. Mary's Sound. However, at 1100, the submarine hit a rock and damage to propellers and hull was incurred in efforts to get off. Excess pressure built up in the inner fuel tank from which oil began to pour into the control, and electric motor compartments. The bulkhead doors had to be closed and soon the men on watch in the control room were splashing about in two or three feet of oil.

The vessel was at a depth of eighty feet, coming up to periscope depth with seven tons of oil and water slopping about in the boat, the Commander was forced to surface in broad daylight.

It was found impossible to dive again, which determined the Commander to set a course at full speed towards the neutral Irish coast in order to abandon ship. However, a Liberator of 103 United States Navy saw him three miles to the west north west of Bishop's Rock. The order to abandon the U Boat was given immediately and some of the crew made a vain attempt to keep the aircraft off by firing the 37 mm gun, while others got out dinghies. The Liberator ran in from astern, straddling the vessel with a stick of depth charges, finishing her off with a second attack in position 49°53'N 06°31'W. Most of the crew were picked out of the water by ships of the Second Escort Group.

Another unusual incident took place in the same month but this time at the northern end of the Irish Sea in a position 55°25'N 06°53'W. U Boat 1003, commanded by Lt. Strübing, managed to return from her first patrol entirely devoid of anything to report. It left Bergen for the second patrol on 18th February, 1945. After schnorkelling for nearly three weeks in the area of the North Channel – again without incident – at 2317 on 20th March, she met up with the alert port look-out on HMCS *New Glasgow*. He reported, *"Low flying aircraft approaching"*, a loud noise not unlike aircraft being heard. Almost immediately afterwards, the same look-out reported, *"Object in the water very close."* In the moonlight, this was identified as a periscope and schnorkel between 50 and 100 yards forward of the port bow – a perfect collision course.

The schnorkel, showing about three feet above water, was partially obscured by a pall of thick yellow smoke. In a matter of seconds, the schnorkel hit the *New Glasgow* immediately below the wing of the bridge. The U Boat crew felt their boat violently shaken and water began to pour into the control room. The Commander ordered a dive to the bottom, there escaping the depth charging which took place through the efforts of the eleven other ships operating with *New Glasgow*.

If Lt. Strübing had shown himself inept by failing to notice the sounds and sights of Naval ships nearby, he proved most enterprising in efforts to save his ship. He lay on the bottom for the rest of that night, keeping the water in check by pumping. He returned to a depth of sixty feet in the morning, cruising until nightfall when he surfaced. By this time, the air in the vessel was foul and batteries very low. He began the task of charging batteries but these efforts were short-lived. Aircraft forced him to dive again with no more than a minimal charge completed. His periscope and schnorkel were beyond repair. He struggled through another day but after midnight on 23rd March the pumps could no longer be kept going. He surfaced and abandoned ship. Next morning thirty one of the crew were picked up by HMCS *Thetford Mines* some fifteen miles north, north west of Inishtrahull.

CHAPTER SIX

Doctor on Board

From the time of commissioning of HMS *Manners* on 16th December, 1943 until her last voyage across the Atlantic to St. John's in Newfoundland we had sailed without more medical assistance than one Sick berth attendant, J Huskie. In November, 1944 Surgeon Lieutenant Michael C. Connell, RNVR joined us, doing so just in time to experience the 1944 hurricane. Like almost all the members of the crew, he was young and untried but when the moment of trial struck found to be more than capable of bearing the strains.

Lieutenant Denis Jermain, our Commanding Officer, had said in his report after the event:

> "The behaviour of the Ship's Company was surprisingly good. Many gloomy forecasts on the probable conduct of such a young crew in an emergency had been made. None of these were fulfilled and this case shows that a young crew with steady Petty Officers is as reliable as any other."

He goes on to commend our Doctor:

> "Surgeon Lieutenant M.C. Connell's attention to the wounded was most praiseworthy. He worked under difficult conditions without regard to his personal safety and saved many lives."

The Doctor's own report makes some of those difficulties more apparent:

> "On the morning of 26th January, 1945 the ship was proceeding up the Irish Sea at a speed of nineteen knots when, at

about 1042, she was hit in the stern by what was evidently an acoustic torpedo. The explosion was not very violent, but it was succeeded by a series of explosions as some of the depth charges, becoming dislodged, rolled into the sea. Gradually, the ship came to a stop but the emergency generators continued to supply power for the lights.

"At the time of the explosion there was a queue for the canteen which is situated to the port side of the laundry flat aft, as it was Stand Easy time. Some of these ratings were injured but it seems likely that, apart from the Canteen Manager and the laundry man, who both had fractured legs, the majority were not severe. These injured ratings started to come forward to the Wardroom which was the pre-arranged main distributing post. Stretcher parties were organised to bring any stretcher cases that there might be to the Wardroom as it was considered that there was no immediate danger of having to abandon ship. The Wardroom was filled with cases, about six in all.

"About fifteen minutes after the first explosion, while the stretcher cases were still being got out of the laundry flat, there was a second and larger explosion. The ship heeled over on her port side but gradually righted herself and remained on an even keel. I went aft after the second explosion and discovered that the stern had been blown off the ship as far as the forrard bulkhead of the Seamen's Mess Deck. The depth charges from the racks on the port and starboard decks had been blown all over the place and were responsible for a number of casualties. The blast, which had mostly been upward in direction, had blown all those standing near the stern into the sea, although a number had been blown up and had landed on the Oerlikon platforms; most of these were dead, either from the blast or the severe injuries sustained on hitting the deck. A few were still alive although severely injured. Some of these casualties, lying on the deck, had been hit by the depth charges. Stretcher parties were organised getting them to the Wardroom after they had been given tubonic Morphia

"The Wardroom was now filled and the Officers' cabins, Captain's cabin and office were all utilised according to the position of the casualty. The Sick Bay itself, which was the after distributing station was unusable as its watertight door was part of the next bulkhead between the Stokers' and Seamen's Mess Deck. This had to remain shut to avert flooding. Fortunately, there was a large emergency chest outside the Petty Officers' Mess which, with the medical stores kept in the Wardroom was adequate for the small amount of dressings that were possible in the short time available.

"Some stock could now be taken of the wounded and it was seen that there were approximately ten severe cases, most of whom had blast injuries as well as a number of fractured femurs and head injuries. Several cases were cyanosed and bleeding from nostrils and mouths and these were evidently cases of blast lungs.

"By now, all the cases had been treated for shock, which mainly consisted in cutting away any wet clothing, covering them with several blackets and giving them morphia and hot drinks if conscious. In the emergency chest there were unfortunately too few hot bottles for the large number of shocked cases.

"A hospital ship – the Atlantis, which was empty and on her way to Liverpool, had been signalled and was now standing by three miles off as there was still, at that time, the possibility that the explosions were due to mines. Three MTBs came alongside and it was possible, as the sea was calm, to have the wounded ferried across to the waiting hospital ship. Although the severe cases might not stand the journey too well on the upper deck of an MTB, it was considered to be the best policy to send all the cases to the hospital ship where medical assistance and transfusions were available, as our damaged ship might be at sea for a further twenty four hours before reaching harbour.

"It was unfortunate that there were only two Thomas splints in the forrard part of the ship, the rest being distributed in the Sick Bay and Medical Store which had been in the stern. This number was not sufficient for the large number of fractured femurs.

"All the wounded had been transferred to the MTBs by two hours after the initial explosion. Now, it was possible to try to clear the dead from the upper deck; but this was found to be extremely difficult as some of the bodies were in the Oerlikon gun wells, having been blown there from below and were now about twelve feet above the iron deck. It was just possible to squeeze a Neal Robertson stretcher between the gun and the edge of the gun well and, having filled it, lower it to the deck below.

"Some of the features of the dead were so distorted as to make them hardly recognisable. The number of fractured Femora was noticeable. There was only one fractured Tibia and Fibula although several fractured wrists and arms."

Any catastrophe must affect those involved with mental changes which can affect them for the rest of life. When that catastrophe causes casualties, like our own, resulting in severe injury and death to one in two of a ship's company – especially when one is responsible for their wellbeing a scar can be carried of which few may be aware.

Our Surgeon Lieutenant had to return to civilian life not long after the events of the 26th January, 1945 as·he was found to be suffering from diabetes. Our Commanding Officer, after receiving his half ring, was posted to command HMS *Duckworth*, another destroyer Escort. This vessel had already seen action off the Lizard and Lands End. On the 24th February, and with the assistance of HMS *Rowley*, U 480. was sunk in a Hedgehog attack. Lt. Förster and all but one of his crew being lost.

This attack took place in 49°59N 6°08'W, which was in the western-most channel between the Scillies and the Seven Stones Light

Vessel. Later *Duckworth* sank U 246 commanded by Lt. Burse this being in position 49°56'N 5°22'. on the 26th March 1945 and on the 29th of the same month U 399 with Lt. Raabe was sunk in position 49°58'N 5°25W. Both of these sinkings had occurred about eight and twelve miles, respectively, to the S.W. of the Lizard Light. The fourth submarine sunk in this area, U 1199 had been on 21st January and brought about by HMS *Icarus* and *Mignonette* after the American Liberty ship, *George Hawley* had been sunk when passing between the Wolf Rock Light and the Longships, a mere mile or so to the west of Lands end.

The Germans had assumed that, after D Day, the Allies would attack on the western coasts of France, attempting to anticipate this by sending a group of submarines to lie in wait. It was these submarines which were being picked off by the Attack groups operating in the area of the western English Channel.

One of the coincidences of life at sea in wartime affected Ronald Bloomfield. In spite of his injuries inflicted by the first Gnat torpedo which hit us, he remembers being carried on board the Motor Torpedo Boat 778 but did not know until years later that he was transferred, thereby, to HS *Atlantis*. He had been a prisoner of war in a Vichy French camp in Langout in North Africa as a result of his ship, HMS Manchester, being sunk on 13th August, 1942. These prisoners of the French were later released and a ship was sent from England to bring them home. This ship, on which Ronald made the voyage home, was the Hospital Ship *Atlantis*!

The story of Stoker First Class Walter Buckley is even more amazing and, to this day, has not been answered to the satisfaction of his wife. His schoolday sweetheart, Mollie, married Walter on the 23rd August, 1940. During 1941, Walter entered the Navy, being eventually drafted to HMS *Manners* in early January, 1945, joining ship in Gladstone Dock in Liverpool. Immediately on joining us, he began his first voyage south to Falmouth and then northwards again to meet our destiny with U 1051. On the 26th January, Mollie received her telegram, "Missing." and a week later, another informing her that

HMS *Aylmer* on the run-in to ram U Boat 1051

(Photo: Sub. Lt. Davies, RNVR)

this had changed to, "Missing, presumed killed."

As Mollie's youngest sister worked in Despatch at the Royal Naval Depot in Oldham, she heard that our wrecked ship had reached Barrow in Furness. They visited the ship, being able to accept the 'Missing' but not the 'Presumed killed.' The Second Lieutenant, Frank Collett, then acting as First Lieutenant, told Mrs. Buckley that Walter was not injured by the first explosion but had been helping the wounded after it. The second torpedo had taken Walter and all working with him in that part of the ship which broke off and sank to the bottom of the Irish Sea. But Mollie has felt, ever since, that her husband was picked up by another ship in a badly wounded state and, without identification being known, taken to a hospital in the United States of America where he died thirty five years later. The episode of the Unknown British Sailor was reported in the American Press, possibly to become the subject of a television programme about Unsolved Mysteries.

The extraordinary coincidence was that this unknown British Sailor picked out of the Atlantic on the 26th January, 1945 had a birth mark on the left side of his chest, this being identical to marks on the chest of Walter Buckley. There was, also, a large scar on the forehead of both Walter and the unknown British Sailor. Walter, of course, had been lost, not in the Atlantic, but in the Irish Sea. Furthermore, no other ship was within sight of *Manners* with the exception of the Hospital Ship *Atlantis*. We were not travelling in company with other ships and the nearest merchant vessel to us was at least fifty miles away; the nearest American ships were the 7,000 ton Liberty Ship, *George Hawley* which was torpedoed near Lands End on the 23rd January, three days before *Manners* was struck and those in the inward bound convoy HX332; two ships of which were sunk on the 27th January just inside St. Georges Channel. There was no-one around us who could have taken Walter aboard an American ship bound for the United States.

The water around *Manners* was scanned very thoroughly, everything on the surface being easily visible to all of us left alive. I recall seeing my own family suit case floating astern of us and marking the position at which we had received the second torpedo. I remembered that this suitcase had been stowed in the bilges of the stern, rueing the fact that it contained my gold watch! Its presence on the water meant that the stern must have broken up right down to the keel before parting from the rest of the hull, filling very quickly with water and sinking.

I remain certain that the only person to have survived being blown over the side into the sea had managed to climb back aboard, when the ship was so far listed to port that the deck was level with the sea. After that, the stern broke loose and the ship righted itself with this survivor uninjured and safely back on deck. Had Walter been floating on that calm sea anywhere between my suitcase and the ship, he would have been clearly visible to us. But how does one explain the coincidence surrounding him, and who was the missing sailor who died in the States in 1980? In the circumstances, how may Mollie receive peace of mind in the knowledge that her husband has been laid to rest? It is not much help to her to know that Walter is listed on Panel 89. Column 3 of the grandiose City War memorial in Portsmouth.

Able Seaman Denis Brown caused some concern to his family seeing him off on the station at the end of his last leave. When he left his father's house in Surbiton to return to Manners, he said to members of his family , *"If I ever lose a limb, I will never come home."* After that sentence, he ran to catch the train, which moved off before he could be overtaken by his father and grandfather. Just after the war, the family had a phone call from Norway, a country in which they knew no-one. The phone was replaced without a word being exchanged. Mr and Mrs. Brown became convinced that Denis had called, having survived the torpedoing. They too, and until the death of Mr. Brown in 1987, remained unable to accept the phrase in that fateful telegram, "Presumed killed." Their nephew, Denis Stanley has continued the unfinished search of his Father, visiting the Records Office in Kew in the hopes that new evidence might have turned up.

Telegraphist D.T. Lockett was drafted from *Manners* to HMS Loch Ruthven a few days before both ships sailed together from Liverpool. He was on watch in the Ship's Radio room when our emergency call came through and he attempted to find out what had happened to his former shipmates. Heresay informed him that *Manners* had been torpedoed north east of the Isle of Man and beached in Scotland. He assumed that this was where the dead were buried. To this day, he retains the unfulfilled desire to visit their graves and pay his respects.

Our distress signal immediately after the second torpedo had struck us was picked up in the Milford Haven Signal Station and the operator on duty happened to be Royal Marine Signalman Maule, the brother, of Stanley Maule, Stoker 1st Class serving in Manners at the time. Signalman Maule knew, therefore, what had happened to his brother's ship. Without saying anything which might breach security, he made busy the telephone lines between Milford Haven and his home in Peebles in his efforts to find out if his brother had figured in any casualty list. As it happened Stanley Maule had survived uninjured.

From South America, Guillermo Jorge Peralta had fulfilled his determination to join up as an Ordinary Seaman in the British Royal Navy. Always cheerful, he was very popular throughout the ship. After the second explosion, he was seen swimming near the ship but disappeared before he could be rescued. His mother started a long correspondence with our Commanding Officer as she had been told by a voodoo soothsayer that her son was still alive. It took many letters to try and convince her that there was no way in which he could have survived. Because of the soothsayer involved, this correspondence became something of a burden, being one of those many cases where the wrong story was concocted in order not to lose a fee!

CHAPTER SEVEN

The Last Stage to Victory

Lieutenant Cremer, one of the few German submariners to have survived five years of war at sea gives the strong impression in his book, *The Story of a U Boat Ace* that every Officer of the German Navy realised, from very early on, that they could not sustain a maritime war against the growing strength of the Allied Navies. For the most part, the surface ships of the Kriegsmarine remained bottled up in the well defended harbours of Germany and the occupied countries and, therefore, submariners were alone.

Certainly, large German warships tested the occasional foray from their home ports, even if only to justify the enormous expense in money, man power and logistical support needed to maintain these vessels. Such attempts ended, all too often, in sinkings and heavy loss of life. The *Admiral Graf Spee* had been lost early on even though it had sailed to the southern hemisphere before hostilities were formally opened in 1939. The largest battle ship ever built, the *Bismarck,* never reached its appointed hunting ground and its cruiser escort, the *Prinz Eugen*, returned, only with difficulty, to its home port in the Baltic. The Allied merchant vessel losses to German surface raiders did not justify the use of these enormous capital ships.

The U Boat alone was the instrument of sinking vast tonnages of Allied merchant shipping and – up to the middle of 1943 – seemed capable of winning the Battle of the Atlantic. Had Germany been able to complete the super submarine which, by the end of 1944, was not yet under production, the story of the War could have been a very different one. This formidable – and for those days – enormous underwater vessel was to be powered by but one type of fuel which could be used both on, and beneath, the surface. Submerged, a designed speed of twenty eight knots was expected, a speed which could be maintained for relatively long periods under water.

Had this submarine become part of the flotillas in the North Atlantic, the Asdics of the day would have been next to useless. Relatively few Allied Naval ships could have carried out attack on a submerged target at more than twenty knots. But, even with this vessel almost ready for operational service, German Naval feeling was that eventually the Allies must win the war at sea.

The year of 1943 has always been looked upon as the one in which the U Boat menace in the Atlantic was brought under control. German Naval codes had been broken, advances had been achieved in high frequency direction finding (HFDF), the perfecting of ship borne radar, especially the Plan Position Indicator (PPI), the use of converted merchant ships as flight decks for anti-submarine planes, even the humble Talk Between Ships (TBS) radio system, all had played a part in the anticipated Allied victory. These appliances meant that the bad old days became memories when the watchkeeper – often even in Atlantic daylight hours – could not see the ship on which station was supposed to be kept.

Captain MacIntyre, DSO and 2 bars, DSC, RN tells us in his book, *U Boat Killer*, that HFDF operators became so proficient that, not only the bearing of a radio transmission but the approximate range as well became known to us. All that an escort needed to do was to dash down a bearing at speed, slowing up at the approximate range so that contact could be established by Asdics. Several submarines were sunk by this method of attack. The German High Command's insistence that U Boats reported their position each day at a precise hour became for them a great weakness. The exchange of radio messages between U Boats acting in a group was found to be a practice too difficult and dangerous. It meant the surfacing of all the U Boats at agreed times. As a result, all messages for a U Boat pack had to originate in Germany and this meant that each U Boat had to report its position even though its transmissions gave instant knowledge to our escorts.

The PPI Radar was capable of pin-pointing a periscope or the protruding two or three feet of a schnorkel. The very first case of this being done was at a range of eight miles by a Canadian Corvette, admittedly in calm sea conditions. Air cover played a vital part, especially when it took place from within the convoy itself. Lt. Cremer tells us that this air cover forced submarines to submerge for the greater part of the twenty four hour day. They could no longer rely on the hours of darkness to allow sufficient time on the surface for their batteries to be recharged and foul air renewed. Crash dives became a frequent occurrence if the U Boat was to have any chance of remaining active on station.

In other words, our naval success with the convoy system was beginning to make life extremely difficult for the submariner and for this reason a new strategy had to be sought. The U Boat fleet gave up the idea of pack hunting on shipping routes across the Atlantic and replaced it with the new method of entry into the shoal waters around the British Isles. Perhaps by this method of attack, ships could be destroyed, once more, in disastrous numbers!

This strategy was seen to fulfil an urgent need as soon as the Invasion of France began in the early June of 1944. Vast tonnages had to be ferried across the English Channel from all the major ports of Britain and, during the several months when the Allied Armies had no more than a couple of Mulberry harbours and a few sandy beaches through which to take delivery, it was an easy task for Admiral Donizt to surmise where his submarines would become most effective.

The Allied Air Forces had commenced their one thousand bomber raids on naval yards, growing shortages of fuel and materials, losses inflicted on the experienced submariner, had all helped to enforce postponement of the delivery date of the first super submarines. They came too late to stave off the inevitable. The war was lost for Germany in much the same way in which the land battle of

1855 in the Crimea was lost by British Naval action taking place in the Baltic – by sea action fought out a long way from opposing land armies. (c/f. *The British Assault on Finland, 1854-1855. A Forgotten Naval War* by Dr. Basil Greenhill and Ann Giffard. The Conway Maritime Press).

For these reasons, the U Boat campaign within the confines of the St. George's and the North Channels the Celtic and Irish Seas took on the appearance almost of a German kamikaze raid. Of the twenty one U Boats known to have operated in that area, a mere three, without damage, found their way home. It became a certainty that the war at sea, initiated by an already insane Hitler and sustained for over five years by blind heroicity of Submariners was finally lost in the Sea nearest to the British Isles.

The day after *Manners* was hit and U 1051 sunk, the medium sized convoy from Halifax, HX 332, entered St. George's Channel. At 0655 it reached a point some fifteen miles to the south of Tuskar Rock Lighthouse on a course of 074°. It had been escorted over the Atlantic by the Canadian Escort Group C7. consisting of HMC Ships *Lanark*, *Hawkesbury*, *Copper Cliff* and *Owen Sound*. It was met off the south of Ireland by the 21st Escort Group consisting of the Captain Class Frigates, HMS *Conn*, *Fitzroy*, *Deane*, *Rupert* and *Redmill*, making nine escorts in all.

Soon after the Bristol Channel section detached at First Light on that morning of the 27th January, 1945 – together with one escort from C7. – HX 332 re-formed into two columns. This manoeuvre was necessary in order that the convoy of some fifteen miles width should become one of six miles across, allowing it to pass more conveniently through mine fields and the restricted inshore waterways of St. George's Channel and the Irish Sea.

The remaining four escorts of C7. formed up ahead of the Convoy while the four vessels of the 21st Escort Group took station on both beams and astern. The new formation settled onto a course of 356°. Immediately after taking up this new course, the convoy was joined by the 5th Escort Group which had come south after the sinking of

The Conning Tower of U Boat 1051, showing damage by the Hedgehog attack of HMS *Bligh*.

(Photo: Sub. Lt. Davies, RNVR)

U 1051 at 1609 on the previous day.

At 1232, the first torpedo struck the sixth ship on its starboard side in the port column of the convoy and two and a half minutes later the second vessel, a tanker and third ship from the rear end of the starboard column, was hit in the port quarter. The two ships involved were the ss. *Ruben Dario* and the tanker ss. *Sölor* and the position was 52°35'N 05°18'W, some forty miles from Tuskar Rock Lighthouse. In other words, the U Boat had managed to manoeuvre between the two columns of the convoy.

The first contact with a submarine echo was achieved a mere two and a half minutes after the second of these explosions. This contact was made by HMS *Rupert* and it was classified as "submarine." This contact was one mile ahead of the second wreck, now drifting in the sea behind the convoy. The position was taken as 'datum' and a dan-buoy was laid so that the remaining ships of the 21st Escort Group could establish a square search with 3 mile sides around the datum point and the 5th Escort Group patrolled an outer square of 6 mile sides. It was then established that the echo heard by *Rupert* was probably a non-sub. and it was abandoned.

During the course of the afternoon, several contacts were investigated and all found to be non-sub. At 1600. it was decided by the Senior Officers to extend the scope of the search. Ships of both Groups were disposed in line abreast, 3,000 yards apart and with a speed of eight knots. They began this new search on a course of 180°. HMS *Tyler* joined the search at 1650. and shortly afterwards, course was altered to 270°. At 2030, at the very western extremity of the search plan, *Keats* obtained a good contact. A Hedgehog attack took place in 45 fathoms of water and five seconds after the projectiles hit the water, there were two explosions. Diesel oil came to the surface and samples for analysis were picked up.

Bottom echoes by echo sounding were obtained and the attack continued but at 2130 contact was lost as though the submarine had broken up as it lay on the bottom. The 21st Escort Group remained in the area for the rest of the night after which the search resumed at daylight on the 28th. Two ships of the 5th Escort Group were able to recover wreckage which rendered the destruction of the U Boat even more certain but the search still continued into the next day, two days after the initial attack on HX.332.

There were no survivors from among the crew of forty six in U 1172. The time was 2008 and the position was 52°24'N 5°42'W, sixteen miles due west of the initial torpedo attack. This meant that the U 1172 was attempting to enter Irish territorial waters – where it would be safe from further attack – but, eight hours after firing its torpedoes, it had been able to travel a mere 16 miles. The wreckage consisted of diesel oil and two inflatables which eventually drifted ashore in Anglesey.

It could be that U 825 commanded by Lt. Cmd Stölker was responsible for the attack on *Ruben Dario* and *Sölor* as he spoke of two explosions being heard after torpedoes had been fired. This submarine managed to return to its homebase undamaged but, after the Armistice on 5th May, 1945, it was taken, together with one hundred other U boats to deep water in the Atlantic and sunk by the British Operation Deadlight.

Of the Captain Class frigates which took part in these attacks, HMS *Redmill* was damaged beyond repair by U 1105 three months later on the 27th April, 1945. The attack took place to the west of Ireland.

When Lt. Jermain left *Manners* to take up his new appointment, it was noticed by the Quartermaster on duty at the gangway, that he saluted for the last time with a very sad and downcast look. He took with him, however, the respect and gratitude of everyone on board. During a well earned period of leave, in which he received his promotion to acting Lt. Commander, he celebrated his marriage to Jean Scott Phillips serving as a signals Officer at Derby House with the rank of Second Officer in the Womens' Royal Naval Service. She was among the first to have seen the signals about the torpedoing of Manners

His new command was HMS *Duckworth*, like *Manners* a Captain

Class Frigate but unlike it in that it was propelled by steam rather than diesel electric. *Duckworth* was already a distinguished ship having assisted in the sinking of U 988 off Lorient on 29th June, 1944. With her new Commander at the age of twenty seven as second-in-command to the Escort Group and her old one acting as Senior Officer, she continued her record with several more attacks and sinkings, finishing with the sinking of U 399. in the English Channel on 26th March 1945.

Duckworth had sailed from Belfast on 11th February to operate under the orders of C-in-C., Plymouth. She was part of the 3rd Escort Group consisting of HMS *Rowley*, *Domett*, *Essington* and *Cooke*. These ships patrolled along the English Channel coast. On the night of the 21st, *Duckworth* and *Cooke* escorted to a safe anchorage in Cawsand Bay two large ships – one of 20,000 tons – which detached from Convoy UC 57A. This was done – with the aid of PPI Radar – at a speed of 10 knots in fog so thick that visibility was cut to never more than half a cable. The Merchant Service Captains of these two ships must have had full confidence in the new electronics of their two escorts.

On the 4th February, the cruiser, HMS *Nyasaland* assisted by the Loch Class sloop, HMS *Loch Scavaig*, working together in the confined waters of the North Channel, attacked and finished off U 1014 commanded by Lt. Glaser. The position was 55°17'N 06°44'W.

The Thames to the Bristol Channel, Convoy BTC 76, lost two ships, probably by the same U Boat 480 under Lt. Förster. *Duckworth* and *Cooke* were on the point of entering Plymouth for a forty eight hour stand-easy. They raced westward to the 'furthest-on' position which was reached at 1505. on 20th February. A hunt was organised with available vessels which consisted of a motley collection of destroyers, frigates, minesweepers and M.Ls as well as a sloop and a trawler! The operation, however, was without success and at dawn on the 24th February, the 3rd Escort Group detached due to fresh U Boat activity to the west of the Longships.

A ship was torpedoed at 0430 just to the west of the Longships

Damaged stern of *Manners*, Barrow-in-Furness outer harbour.　(Photo: Sub. Lt. David Gibson, RNVR)

Lighthouse in Convoy BTC 78, travelling from the Thames to Bristol. The U Boat Captain – according to the Ministry of Defence War Diary, showed himself to be cool and very skilful in the handling of his vessel. He discharged bubble targets while continuing on his southerly course, keeping about twenty to thirty feet above the sea bed. At midday, he managed to throw off his pursuers from the scent until *Duckworth* regained it and ran in for the final attack. The U Boat 'bottomed' during the run-in and after being attacked, only a small amount of oil came to the surface. *Rowley* made a further attack with Hedgehogs and this brought up a considerable amount of wreckage. *Duckworth* continued the attack with depth charges and a widespread area of oil appeared together with several brand new, but very battered, tins of German dried egg, several fresh loaves of bread, a forage cap complete with a Nazi badge, a lot of splintered wood and some fragments of what looked like plastic material.

Lt. Commander Jermain, in his Western Approaches Memories, gives revealing clues about the way in which U Boats were hunted around the Scilly Isles and the Wolf Rock Lighthouse:

"Our Group had the task of hunting in coastal waters for the schnorkel boats which had started to be a serious threat to coastal convoys. They would lie close to rocks or wrecks where their echoes would be hard to distinguish, coming to periscope depth only when a convoy passed. After attacking, they would again merge into the background. The aim of the Support Groups was to get to know their areas, in our case the Western Channel and around the Cornish peninsula.

"One evening, we knew that a convoy was due to round Land's End the next morning. After studying the chart we deduced the position where the submarine would choose to wait and the time it would attack. Precisely on cue, a small coaster was hit and we went straight to our chosen position where the submarine was detected before it could get to safety. The first salvo hit and we had two survivors on board within twenty minutes of the torpedo hitting.

"There was a typical sailors' reaction towards the survivors. When they first surfaced, the bloodlust was up and the guns' crews had to be restrained from firing. By the time we were alongside, the reaction had set in and the men had to be restrained from jumping overboard in their zeal to help. 'They are only some mothers' sons' was the cry. When one of the Germans died, a sense of gloom ran through the ship."

On the 7th March, our Canadian friends in Escort Group C7, HMCS La Hulloise, Strathadam and Thetford Mines, successfully attacked and sank U 1302 commanded by Lt. Herwarzt in 52°19'N 05°23'W. This position was not more than a quarter of the distance between Strumble Head in Wales and Tuskar Rock off the coast of Ireland and a little to the south of where HX 332 had been attacked at the end of January.

Lt. Gebauer's command of U 681 came to an end on 11th March with an attack from the air by VPB-103. (Very long range patrol bomber) It occurred just a little further to the west as though this U Boat had begun to await ships circling the Scilly Isles rather than risk the persisting U Boat activity in the various channels between the Isles and the Longships Lighthouse.

Telegraphist D.T. Lockett had been drafted from *Manners* just prior to our sailing from Liverpool on 5th January for our last voyage. He joined HMS *Loch Ruthven* and sailed from Liverpool just behind us. It was this Loch Class Frigate which figured successfully against U 638 on 12th March, 1945. Assisted by *Wild Goose*, Lt. Keller's U Boat was sunk, again within sight of Land's End in position 49°52'N 05°52'W.

A U Boat sinking took place in the seaward end of the North Channel. On the 20th March, HMCS *New Glasgow* caught Lt. Strübing unawares and managed to sink U 1003 at 55°25'W 06°40W. While in the south, the Thames to Bristol Convoy BTC 81, lost a single ship in very thick fog. No one realised that a torpedoing had occurred until the Escort astern of the convoy encountered the ship, stopped and sinking. The submarine responsible was not detected.

Aircraft achieved a sinking in the North Channel on the 22nd March when Br. Sqdn 120 managed to attack and sink U 296 commanded by Lt. Rasch in the position 55°23'N 06°40W. This was followed on the 26th March in the south to the south west of the Lizard. *Duckworth*, using the growing knowledge of U Boat tactics around the rock strewn area of Cornwall and the Scilly Isles, attacked Lt. Buhse commanding U 246 managing to sink it at 49°56'N 05°22'W.

Lt. Cmd. Jermain says of this attack:

> "The Group's Senior Officer, Ronnie Mills had moved temporarily to a sister ship and I was sniffing around a pinnacle of rock off the Lizard and thought I had a good contact which could have been the rock or a U Boat. After an hour or so, the contact began to move up-tide so I gave it a pattern of Hedgehog and got some explosions a short way under water indicating the probability of a kill. No oil nor debris came to the surface so no claim could be made. After the War, German records showed that a submarine had been lost in the area so I got Their Lordships' pleasure by post; the same post brought an expression of their displeasure on another matter – surely a record!"

On the 27th March, 1945, a ship which had come from the Thames to Bristol Convoy BTC 81 detached in order to join the Halifax Convoy ONA 287. At 0930, this vessel was torpedoed between the two convoys. Revenge however, was swift and sure. U 1018 under Lt. Burmeister was sunk with all hands by HMS *Loch Fada* in a position just to the south of Land's End, 49°56'N 05°20'W and, by that evening U 327 under Lt. Lemcke was sunk by HMS *Labuan*, *Loch Fada* and *Wild Goose*, again just to the south of Land's End, at 49°46'N 05°47'W.

HMS *Teme*, the last escort sloop to be torpedoed during the Battle in the Irish Sea area was attacked off Falmouth on the 29th March, the submarine managing to elude destruction.

Two final penetrations through the North Channel and reaching as far south as 52°03'N 05°53'W – about twenty five miles north of St. David's Head – ended in the sinkings of U 1169 on 5th April and U 1024 on 12th April. The first of these involved Lt. Goldbeck's Unterseeboot striking a mine and sinking without survivors. The second was the capture of U 1024, commanded by Lt. Gutteck, by HMS *Loch Glendu*. This submarine was taken in tow by an assisting Loch Class sloop, HMS *Loch More* but sank while under tow at position 53°39'N 05°03'W. The crew was taken prisoner.

The last action of the Battle in the Irish Sea took place on 16th April 1945. HMS *Loch Killin* detected, attacked and sank Lt. Stephan's U 1063. The U Boat battle ended in a position, again adjacent to but just to the north of Land's End in 50°08'N 05°52'W. The European War ended with the unconditional surrender of Germany on the 12th May, 1945, just twenty six days later.

During those last weeks of the War, nineteen submarines were lost within the confines of the Irish Sea, which means that, with an average crew of 46 men, some eight hundred and fifty submariners gave their lives heroically for the lost cause of that German tyrant who did not have the courage to account for his crimes.

Appendix One

BRITISH CASUALTIES SUFFERED
ON 26th. JANUARY, 1945

K 568. HMS *MANNERS*

A.B.	Albert Frederick	ADAMS	P/JX 275449
A.B.	Herbert William	ANGOLD	P/JX 189272
Sto.	Albert	ABBOTT	P/KX 105388
A.B.	Albert	ATTREE.	P/JX 624852
A.B.	Frederick Antony	BANNING	P/JX 624910
P.O.	William	BARSDELL	P/JX 125805
O/Tel.	Phillip Harry	BARNLEY	P/JX 817840
A.B.	Sidney	BLACKWELL	P/JX 518474
A.B.	Dennis Raymond	BROWN	P/JX 518171
A.B.	James	BUSH	P/JX 630322
Sto.	Walter	BUCKLEY	P/KX 119868
Sto.	John	BUTCHER	P/KX 602569
Lt.	J.C.	CARTER	R.N.V.R
A.B.	William	CHEAL	P/JX 624923
P.O.	Edward George	COLLARD	MMC/MX 621195
Lt.	D.W.	COLLINS	R.N.V.R
O/Sig.	Frank	CRANAGE	P/JX 713682
Sto.	Harry	CROSS	P/KX 602485
A.B.	Noel	DELOOZE	P/JX 624933
S/Lt.	George	GLYNN	R.N.V.R
A.B.	Ronald Henry	GRUBB	P/JX 625854
A.B.	Frederick	HARDY	P/JX 624849
Sto.	Francis	HILL	P/JX 597816,
A.B.	James	KNOTT	P/JX 625853
A.B.	Albert Sidney	LEDGER	P/JX 624937
A.B.	Robert	LEGGET	C/DX 2549
Sig.	Robert	McMILLAN	NXD 4044
A.B.	William	MEREDITH	P/JX 625570

A.B.	Richard John	NEVE	P.JX 385946
A.B.	David	NICKLESS	P/JX 630314
A.B.	Thomas	NOLAN	P/JX 262796
E.R.A.	Thomas	NORRIS	P/MX 58964
O/S.	Guillermo Jorge	PERALTA	P/JX 633687
P.O.	Arthur Francis	PIERREPOINT	P/JX 14173
A.B.	Colin	PICKERING	P/JX 363363
A.B.	Stanley Bernard	PYM	P/JX 624933
L/Sea.	Thomas	REW	U/DX 1331
Canteen Manager	William	RIBCHESTER	C/MX 583288
Lt.(E).	E.	RICHES	RNR
L/Sto.	Francis	VALLANCE	P/KX 119847
Sto.	Frederick	WATERS	P/KX 105388
A.B.	Derek	WILSON	P/JX 155296
A.B.	Donald Edward	WOOD	P/JX 275449.

These forty three souls lie at rest, thirty seven with their ship, HMS *Manners* in position 53°29.5'N. 05°09'W. that is 280° 21 milesfrom The Skerries Light north of Anglesey, three with Military honours in cemeteries listed below and three in family graves in their home towns

INJURED

A.B.	Ronald Leslie	BLOOMFIELD	P/JX 323113
A.B.	Walter	BRENNAN	P/JX 358440
L/Sto.	John	CARTER	P/KX 100516
A.B.	Desmond	CASTLE	P/JX 624908
A.B.	Albert	EWINS	D/JX 419716
A.B.	Charles	GRANT	P/JX 263597
A.B.	Clifford Charles	HARFORD	P/JX 296647
A.B.	Roger	HAYFORD	P/JX 521883
O.S.	Daniel	HOLDCROFT	P/JX 639868
A.B.	Leonard	HUNT	P/JX 565953
A.B.	Leslie	LOTE	P/JX 624896

Sto.	Joseph	McINTYRE	P/KX 165899
A.B.	Ronald	TODD	P/JX 624850
L/Sto.	John	VEITCH	P/KX 103583

SLIGHTLY INJURED

| Sto. | Joseph | STEPHENSON | P/KX 596715 |

BURIED WITH FULL MILITARY HONOURS

Frederick HARDY in the Town Cemetery at Bromley at Kent
Robert McMILLAN in the Barrow in Furness Town Cemetery
        3rd. February, 1945
        Grave No. 2125-5-A Section 5
Frederick WATERS in the Barrow in Furness Town Cemetery
        3rd. February, 1945
        Grave No. 2589-11-A Section 11

These graves are maintained by the WAR GRAVES COMMISSION and headstones are inscribed with the Navy Crest, Rank and the name of H.M.S. Manners

APPENDIX TWO.

GERMAN CASUALTIES SUFFERED ON
26th. JANUARY, 1945

U-BOOT 1051

Kommandant: ObLt.z.S Heinrick von HOLLEBEN commanding a crew of forty eight men

MtrOGfr.	Otto	ALBERN	27.11.24
FkOGfr.	Günter	ALBERT	30.05.25
OBtsMt.	Kurt	ANDERS	14.01.22
OBtsMt.	Walter	ANDERS	19.01.22
MtrOGfr.	Kurt	ANTHECK	13.02.24
MtrOGfr.	Hans	ANTWEILER	08.05.25
MtrOGfr.	Alfred	AUGUSTINIACK	20.03.24
MtrOGfr.	Franz	BAUMANN	10.06.25
FkOGfr.	Hans-Joachim	BIESEKE	29.09.24
MechGfr.	Karl-Heinz	BRÖDLING	29.05.25
StOStrm.	Wilhelm	CLEMENT	13.03.15
FkMt.	Walter	DÖHLER	06.05.21
MtrOGfr.	Josef	EDER	10.12.25
MaschMt.	Heinrick	EGELHOF	23.05.22
MaschMt.	Heinrick	EMPTE	03.07.20
Lt.	Kurt-Walter	ENKE	29.01.24
Mtr.	Gerhard	ERFURTH	31.07.25
MaschOGfr	Hans	GRÖF	09.01.24
MechOGfr.	Karl	HAGENLOCHER	19.08.22
OMasch.	Phillipp	MAX	21.04.17
OLt.	Hans-Gunter	HENKE	20.03.23
MaschHGfr.	Helmut	HÖLZER	27.05.20
OLt.	Heinrick von	HOLLEBEN	13.03.19
MaschMt.	Georg	KÄFER	11.03.20
MechOGfr.	Herbert	KEMMING	29.05.24

OMasch.	Kurt	KIENE	09.04.17
Lt (Ing).	Wolfgang	KNOTHE	10.12.22
MaschGfr.	Martin	KOCH	23.06.24
MaschMt.	Peter	NOACK	17.01.20
MaschHGfr.	Werner	PETZOLDT	20.03.22
MaschOGfr.	Heinz	PSZOLLA	14.08.23
MaschMt.	Heinz	SCHMITZ	18.06.23
OFkMt.	Willi	SCHRÖER	27.09.18
MaschOgfr.	Heinrick	SCHWEEN	23.04.24
MaschOGfr.	Werner	SITTNER	14.12.22
BtsMt.	Heinz	TEUBER	26.11.21
MtrOGfr.	Anton	TÖPPER	13.06.26
MaschOGfr.	Erich	VALENTIN	09.06.24
MtrOGfr.	Heinz	WALD	14.11.23
OMechMt.	Fritz	WEBER	10.08.19
MtrOGfr.	Johannes	WEBER	04.04.22
FkOGfr.	G'nter	WEICK	13.01.24
MtrOGfr.	Karl	WEIDMANN	23.10.23
MaschMt.	Ernst	WEISER	14.10.21
OSanMt.	Willy	WEIBER	26.02.20
OLt.	Erich	WIEKER	11.04.12
MaschOGfr.	Otto	WILLENBERG	23.02.23
OBtsMT.	Heinz	BALK	29.01.22

These forty eight souls lie at rest in their submarine in position
53°39'N 05°23'W.

APPENDIX THREE

GERMAN CASUALTIES SUFFERED ON
27th. JANUARY, 1945

U-BOOT 1172

Kommandant: ObLt.z.S. JÙrgen KUHLMANN commanding a crew of forty six men

MechMt.	Manfred	ARNOLD	21.04.24
MtrOGfr.	Franz	BAUER	24.03.24
OBtsMt.	Josef	BAUER	19.10.19
MaschOGfr.	Walter	BENDER	20.12.24
MaschGfr.	Heinrich	BERG	24.10.25
MaschMt.	Heinz	BEYERSDORF	28.11.23
FkMt.	Manfred	BÖCKENKROGER	02.07.21
MaschOGfr.	Alfons	BÜTTNER	02.10.24
MaschOGfr.	Wilhelm	DICKS	11.02.25
FkOGfr.	Friedrich	FISCHER	24.02.24
OStrm.	Karl	GEHMAIR	11.12.18
MtrOGfr.	Josef	GIESBERTZ	30.04.25
MtrOGfr.	Willi	GLATZ	26.02.25
MaschOGfr.	Karl-Heinz	GOLLOJUCH	04.03.24
MaschGfr.	Josef	GRÖNHAUT	07.03.21
FkMt.	Ernst	HAMMER	29.09.22
MtrOGfr.	Herbert	HEINZ	06.05.24
MtrGfr.	Hermann	HELLE	09.06.25
OMasch	Hugo	HOLST	02.07.20
MaschMt.	Erich	JENA	07.09.22
MtrOGfr.	Robert	JUNG	23.08.24
MtrGfr.	Walter	JURASCHEK	09.12.25
OMasch.	Jakob	KIEFER	03.02.15
MaschMt.	Hans	KIEFER	21.07.24
OLt.	Jürgen	KUHLMANN	03.03.20

Lt(Ing).	Anton	KUNZ	24.05.22
OStrm.	Gerhard	LENZ	04.06.16
MaschMt.	Gustav	MENKE	04.12.21
MtrOGfr.	Paul	MIKOLAICZYK	13.04.24
MechGfr.	Gert-Rainer	MÜLLER	30.07.25
MaschMt.	Horst	NEUMANN	24.08.22
MtrHGfr.	Walter	OPITZ	25.07.23
OBtsMt.	Ludwig	OSKAMP	16.03.21
MaschOGfr.	Wilhelm	OSTERKAMP	11.12.21
OSanMt.	Heinz	OSTERMANN	01.02.20
MtrGfr.	Karl	OSTERTAG	04.04.25
MaschOGfr.	Josef	PFEIFER	24.04.25
Lt.	Helmut	RAEDER	30.05.23
MaschHGfr	Bruno	RAMBAUSKE	23.05.21
MtrOGfr.	Bruno	RIEMER	19.01.25
MechGfr.	Rudi	RÖPER	18.06.24
FkOGfr.	Willi	ROHDE	25.11.20
MechGfr.	Willi	ROMAHN	17.11.24
FkOGfr.	Hermann	SCHÖN	21.04.20
MaschMt.	Erich	SCHWINGER	21.10.21
MaschOGfr.	Franz	SEILER	23.12.24

These forty seven souls lie at rest in their Submarine in position
52°24'N 05°42'W.

APPENDIX FOUR

WESTERN APPROACHES MEMORIES
Captain Denis Jermain, DSC., RN.

After four years in MTBs, I was greatly surprised to be appointed to command HMS *Manners*, a Captain Class diesel-electric Destroyer Escort. Until then, I had, literally, never been to sea in anything between a ten thousand ton cruiser and an MTB. It was with some trepidation that I started a round of courses, but I found that my experience covered much of the routine problem of command and one's basic training coped with the technical side. Convoy tactics on the other hand were a new subject. However, a course at the Western Approaches Tactical Unit under Captain Roberts worked wonders. I have always felt that his contribution towards winning the Battle of the Atlantic by teaching convoy tactics to beginners has never received adequate recognition.

It was while I was doing my tactical course that the first attack on a convoy by submarines firing acoustic torpedoes (GNATS) was made. Within twenty four hours of the first report, Captain Roberts had devised the Step Aside procedure which became the standard tactical method for escorts to get within attacking range of a submarine fitted with GNATS. This alone deserved the gratitude of all at sea.

To my consternation, when I arrived at Boston Navy Yard in early November, 1943 to stand by my ship that was due for completion before Christmas, I was told to go away as assembly would not start for a fortnight. In the event she was commissioned on 17th. December and sailed in the first week of January, 1944. The pace of activity was exemplified by the way gangs of welders (all female) would patrol the ship at night looking for fittings to be welded into place, indicated by a chalk mark saying, Weld. During embarkation of ammunition, the depth charges had been left on deck overnight. Each British depth charge has a stencilled sign reading Weld, here indicating the join in the casing where the two parts meet. The inevitable happened and the next morning we found all our depth charges firmly welded to the upper deck.

From Boston, we sailed to Casco Bay in Portland, Maine in mid-winter for sufficient familiarisation to get to Bermuda for a work-up before joining a convoy across the Atlantic. Just south of the Azores, one of the shafts snapped and I had to crawl for the rest of the way on one shaft at a speed slow enough to avoid risking it going the way of the other: most nerve-wracking. This was due to an inherent defect in the diesel electric ships which was cured by fitting an extra 'A' bracket to stop the shaft from whipping. Apart from this and the excess stability of the ships that made them roll far too much owing to the reduction in gun armament by the British (cured by fitting larger bilge keels and carrying many more depth charges on deck), the Captain class ships were ideal for their task and compared very favourably with anything else in the Atlantic except the converted destroyers. It was indeed lucky for me and many other learners that the Admiralty had not appreciated this fact and had sent us to these ships while much more senior and deserving officers were being given home grown Loch Class and other frigates which were much less effective.

One of the major benefits in the Captain Class was the operations room that had a plotting table and high definition radar. This meant that we conduct virtually everything from there: the shape of things to come, but revolutionary at the time.

Being such a junior boy, I was shunted between escort groups to fill gaps and therefore saw little of any one Group Commander for the first year except for John Wasterhouse who ran a multi-national group of Norwegian, Belgium and British ships with great energy and, believe it or not (If you ever knew John well) tact. Sadly, one calm night my Officer of the Watch and that of the Norwegian Ship *Rose* got themselves into a muddle and ended up with the bows of *Manners* in the engine room of *Rose*. So calm was the sea that all but one of Rose's crew were saved.

By this time, Autumn 1944, attacks on convoys had dwindled and the glory was passing to the Support Groups who had freedom to hunt submarines away from the convoys. Nevertheless, the perils of the sea were ever present. One convoy that included landing ships and craft left the Irish Sea in a flat calm and met a sudden storm in the night. At dawn, the sea was littered with capsized ships and landing craft. For the escorts there was little they could do to help as they had their own problems in surviving. This was another occasion when captains had to decide whether to advise crews in distress to stay with their hulks or to abandon ship. Both methods ended in tragedy.

I well remember one slow convoy whose Commodore's noon position went astern on successive days! After some of these slow convoys the ship's company was suffering so much from colds and boils that I suggested we should be given a daily ration of canned fruit juice. After scorn by the doctors, the Governor of Newfoundland, Admiral Walwyn, prompted by Lady Walwyn, took the point and persuaded them to approve. The result was miraculous with scarcely a sniffle from then on.

With my frequent moves from Group to Group so I changed from Base to Base. Each had its own qualities for recreation and support but all had the benefit of the dedicated Wren Staff. Time and again equipment problems that had defeated the men would be solved by Wren maintainers who were unstinting in the hours they worked in order to ensure that we sailed with everything working.

One particular Wren Officer for whom all Commanding Officers had a grateful spot in their hearts was Kay Halloran, an American and Flag Lieutenant to the C in C. who sadly died soon after the War. People like me who, as beginners, were prone to make mistakes would have frequent summonses to Max Horton to explain their misdeeds. Kay, with her great charm, would calm the anxious and soothe the chastened and is another unsung personality of the Command. Fortunately, I was advised that Max had remarked after one of my visits that at least my sins were those of commission and not inaction. He was unforgiving to the latter.

Poor *Manners* came to a sad end. While on passage up the Irish Sea, which had always been considered free from U Boats, she was hit by a GNAT torpedo fired by the first of the snorkel submarines to have penetrated so far inshore. Both shafts were broken and after she was stopped a second torpedo hit the stern where the damage control parties were assembled. Casualties, which included over forty men killed, were high but, although some twenty feet of the stern had been sheared off, the rest of the ship was intact. Not a drop of water entered and not a light bulb broke which speaks highly for the design and of the all-welded construction that had received so much scorn until then. The Asdic team got their set working and the U Boat was detected some 1,500 yards away. There it stayed for a couple of hours until a support group came along and I was able to give them the submarine's position. An immediate attack brought her to the surface where she was promptly rammed by the Senior Officer (Bertram Taylor) I don't think the C in C. was too happy to have lost the chance of capturing a snorkel boat and to have had yet another escort put our of action.

The crew during this rather gruesome experience was magnificent despite forebodings that such a young lot, of whom the 26 year old Captain was about the oldest, would crumble under pressure. The secret lay in an excellent Coxswain and very good Petty Officers who were, if anything, older than average and had had plenty of war experience.

Manners was paid off very soon after and her hull towed to Greece where her machinery provided power for Athens. After a brief leave I was sent to command HMS *Duckworth*, another Captain Class but with steam machinery, to take over from Commander Ronnie Mills who remained on board as Support Group Commander. Experience had shown that Group Commanders, especially in Support Groups were too hard pressed to command their own ships and also needed to move from ship to ship as the situation required.

Our group had the task of hunting in coastal waters for the snorkel boats who had started to be a serious threat to coastal convoys. They would lie close to rocks or wrecks where their echoes would be hard to distinguish, coming to periscope depth only when a convoy passed. After attacking, they would again merge into the background. The aim of the support groups was to get to know their areas, in our case the western Channel and waters around the Cornish peninsula.

One evening, we knew that a convoy was due to round Land's End the next morning. After studying the chart we deduced the position where the submarine would choose to wait and the time it would attack. Precisely on cue a small coaster was hit and we went straight to our chosen position where the submarine was detected before it could get to safety. The first salvo hit and we had two survivors on board within twenty minutes of the torpedo hitting. We fully conceded that the influence of Captain Robert's tactical training was guiding us.

There was a typical sailors' reaction towards the survivors. When they first surfaced, the bloodlust was up and the guns' crews had to be restrained from firing. By the time we were alongside, the reaction had set in and the men had to be restrained from jumping overboard in their zeal to help. *"They are only some mothers' sons"* was the cry. When one of the Germans died, a sense of gloom ran through the ship. I am sure that this was an oft-repeated feature of the war at sea. Certainly in MTBs there was a common sense of sympathy between small craft sailors of all navies.

Shortly after this, when Ronnie Mills had temporarily moved to a sister ship, I was sniffing around a pinnacle rock off the Lizard and thought I had a good contact which could have been the rock or a U Boat. After an hour or so, the contact began to move up-tide so I gave it a pattern of Hedgehog and got some explosions a short way under water indicating the probability of a kill. No oil nor debris came to the surface so no claim could be made. After the War, German records showed that a submarine had been lost in the area so I got Their Lordships pleasure by post; the same post that brought an expression of their displeasure on another matter - surely as record!

An unusual feature of these coastal operations was in coming to terms with fatigue. After a hunt lasting forty eight hours around headlands and into bays one just had to take a stretch off the land for eight hours to get enough rest to resume. Hence, presumably the nautical expression.

The war was now approaching its end and we began to feel on top of the threat posed by inshore U Boats, but we knew that the next generation with much higher under-water speeds was on its way; indeed one of our group reckoned he had already met such a one, greatly to his embarrassment. No doubt we would have developed tactics in time particularly as co-operation with Coastal Command was steadily improving.

VE Day found us anchored off Bembridge and the Senior Officer decided to show the sailors what peace-time routine was like. After a forenoon of general drill and an afternoon of training classes, everyone was thankful when it became apparent that the U Boats had not received the good news and we were sent out to resume patrolling in our restful war-time routine!

Although I had arrived in Western Approaches after the horrors of the convoy battles, I did get action of a very different kind. We, the warships, became the targets, and our technical equipment and weapons, which improved enormously in the final year, were hard-pressed to keep pace with the threat which had now turned against coastal convoys and which could have become almost as dangerous if peace had not arrived before the faster U Boats.

APPENDIX FIVE

THE VOYAGES OF HMS *MANNERS*

1944

Jan 5th	Sailed for Casco Bay
10th	Sailed for Bermuda
13th	Arrived Grassy Bay
Feb 14th	Sailed for Liverpool. 1st Eastbound
	Lost the port prop. shaft
Mar 1st	Arr. Gladstone dock
	Refit in Birkenhead
Apr	Refit in Birkenhead
May	Refit in Birkenhead
June 15th	Sailed for Campeltown Asdic Course
27th	Sailed for the Minches
July 2nd	Arr Larne for work up
6th	Sailed for Naples
17th	Arr Naples
19th	To Pozzuoli
25th	Sailed for Gladstone Dock
Aug 4th	Arr Liverpool
10th	Sailed for Larne
15th	Sailed for St. John's. 1st Westward crossing
27th	Arr St. John's
Sept 4th	Sailed for Liverpool. 2nd Eastbound
15th	Arr. Gladstone Dock.
23rd	Sailed for St. John's. 2nd Westward crossing
Oct 14th	Sailed for Liverpool. 3rd Eastbound
23rd	Arr. Gladstone dock
Nov 8th	Sailed for Larne. 4 days work up
13th	FRIDAY sailed with ONO 260. 3rd. Westward
	Hurricane. Surg. Lieut, Connell's first trip
26th	Hit HMCS *Rose*. 13th Day out. 0030. Left convoy
Dec 1st	Arr St. John's
3rd	Sailed for Bay Bulls Slip. 8 days

Dec	11th Unslipped and sailed to St. John's
18th	Sailed for Liverpool. 4th Eastbound
25th	Mid Atlantic. Tubby Matthews sports his Christmas Tree and we serenade the convoy.
30th	Arr. Gladstone Dock

1945

Jan	5th Sailed for Falmouth
7th Arr	Falmouth. Hit by Tug dragging anchor. Dry dock
25th	Sailed for Liverpool
26th	Torpedoed 1042. 280° 21 miles Skerries Lt

Number of Atlantic crossings: 4 Eastbound	= 12,000 n.s.m.. approx
3 Westward	= 9,000
Return voyage to Minches etc	= 1,200
Return voyage to NAPLES	= **6,000**
TOTAL DISTANCE RUN	**28,000**. approx
Pitometre Log reading at end	**32,000**. n.s.m.

APPENDIX SIX

BATTLE IN THE IRISH SEA

SEQUENCE OF PRINCIPLE EVENTS, NOVEMBER, 1944 TO MAY 1945

1944

1st Nov 44	U 483 torpedoed HMS *Whittaker* off Malin Head. No Officer survived and casualties were very heavy. Towed to Belfast
11th	U 1200 Lt. Mangels sunk by *Pevensey Castle*, *Launceston Castle*, *Portchester Castle* and *Kenilworth Castle*. 50°24'N 09°10'W.
17th Dec	U 400 Lt. Creutz sunk by *Nyasaland*.

THE FATEFUL JANUARY 1945

15th Jan	U 1055 Lt Meyer sank MT Maja 8000t.53°40'N05°14'W
15th	HMS *Thane*, Aircraft Carrier torpedoed and damaged beyond repair off the Clyde by U 482
16th	U 482 Lt. von Matuscha sunk by *Starling*, *Peacock*, *Hart*, 55°30'N 05°53'W, North Channel.
21st	U 1199 Lt. Stollmann sank Liberty Ship, *George Hawley* 7,176t.1448hrs.50°N 05° 45'W. Convoy TBC 43 (Thames to Bristol).
21st	*Icarus* and *Mignonette* sank U 1199 Lt. Stollmann 49°57'N 5°42'W.
21st Jan	U 1172 Lt. Kuhlmann sank ms *Galatea*, 1,152t 52°40'N. 5°23'W. Sole survivor picked up on 22nd. by *Tyler* 22 miles WSW Bardsey Isle.
23rd Jan	U 1051 sank ms. *Vigsnes* 1,599t. 53°33'N 4°17'W. at 1645. (Cardiff to Mersey detached from Convoy MH1). All crew landed from own boats.
25th Jan	1600hr *Manners* sailed from Falmouth. Zig-zag No. 8.
26th	0630 altered co. to investgate contact. 0830. Sighted two lifeboats *Galatea*, Bergen

52°54'N 5°20'W.

1042 MANNERS hit by first torpedo. 280° 21 miles Skerries Lt.

1055 second hit by torpedo. HS *Atlantis* assists.

1230 MTBs 778, 767, 765 arrive from Holyhead.take wounded to Atlantis.

U 1051 Lt. Holleben. 1609 sunk by *Aylmer, Calder* and *Bentinck* assisted by *Bligh.* 5th EG. 53°39'N 5°21'W.

Bligh goes south to assist HX 332.

27th   HX 332 Convoy from Halifax to UK (Liverpool) enters Irish Sea in the south.

1232 First attack on HX 332. in position 20 miles SW. Bardsey isle. 52°35'N. 05°18'W.

5th. Escort Group engages sub contact assisted by 21st. EG.

5th and 21st continue attack until 29th. January.

U 1172, Lt. Kuhlmann sunk by *Keats, Tyler* and *Bligh.* 52°24'N 5°42'W. Diesel oil and two inflatables sighted, later drifted ashore in Anglesey.

U 825 Lt. Cmd Stölker sank MT *Solör* 8,200t. and *Ruben Dario* 7,100t. 52°35'N 5°18'W.

This submarine managed to return to its homebase undamaged but, after the Armistice on 5th. May, 1945, it was taken, together with one hundred other U boats to deep water in the Atlantic and sunk by the British Operation Deadlight.

THE FINAL DAYS OF THE WAR IN THE IRISH SEA

4th Feb   U 1014 Lt. Glaser sunk 55°17'N 06°44'W. by *Loch Scavaig, Nyasaland.*

20th Feb   U 1208 Lt. Hagene sunk 51°48'N 07°07'W. by *Amethyst*

22nd Feb   At 1330. Two ships in Convoy BTC.76 torpedoed in the Coastal Channel off Falmouth.

24th Feb   0430 One ship in Convoy BTC.78. torpedoed off the Longships Lighthouse.

U 480 Lt. Förster sunk 49°55'N 06°08'W by *Duckworth,*

	Rowley.
27th Feb	At 0930 one ship detaching from Convoy BTC 81. to join ONA 287. was torpedoed
	U 1018 Lt. Burmeister sunk 49°56'N 05°20'W. by *Loch Fada*
	U 327 Lt. Lemcke sunk 49°46'N 05°47'W. by *Labuan, Loch Fada, Wild Goose.*
7th Mar	U 1302 Lt. Herwartz sunk 52°19'N 05°23'W. by HMCS *La Hulloise, Strathadam, Thetford Mines.*
11th Mar	U 681 Lt. Gebauer sunk 49°53'N 06°31'W. by VPB-103.
12th Mar	U 638 Lt. Keller sunk 49°52'N 05°52'W by *Loch Ruthven, Wild Goose.*
20th Mar	U 1003 Lt. Strübing sunk 55°25'N 06°40'W. by HMCS *New Gladgsow.*
21st Mar	One ship torpedoed in Convoy BTC.81. in fog.
22nd Mar	U 296 Lt.Rasch sunk 55°23'N 06°40'W. by Br. Sqdn 120.
26th Mar	U 246 Lt. Buhse sunk 49°56'N 05°22'W by *Duckworth.*
29th Mar	HMS *Teme*, Sloop, torpedoed off Falmouth.
5th Apr	U 1169 Lt. Goldbeck. sunk by mine with no survivors 52°03'N 05°53'W..
12th Apr	U 1024 Lt. Gutteck. Captured by HMS *Loch Glendu.* Towed by *Loch More* but sank underway. 53°39'N 05°03'W.
16th Apr	U 1063 Lt. Stephan. sunk by HMS *Loch Killin.* 50°08' 05°52'W. This was the last action in which a submarine was sunk in the Irish Sea or its environs.

During these last weeks of the War, nineteen submarines were lost within the confines of the Irish Sea which means that with an average crew of 46 men, some eight hundred and seventy five submariners gave their lives heroically for the lost cause of that German tyrant. In the same period, many more U Boats were lost along the west coast of Scotland, the English Channel and to the west of Ireland.

ACKNOWLEDGEMENTS

May I record my gratitude to the following sources by which I was able to check details of fact which, through failing memory, might have become distorted

Commanding Officer's Report on damage to Manners. P.01254/45 Appendix to Letter 696/13. 31.1.45.

Western Approach Memories. Capt. Denis Jermain, DSC, RN.

WAR DIARY. Home Command 26.1.45. Friday.

No. W.A. 549/0202/11/30. HMS *Grindall* report of proceedings

Mr. Eddie Hale. *Hoist the Jolly Roger* The story of D.E. Groups 1943-45.

Surg. Lieut. M.C. Connell, RNVR. Report on Casualties.

Mr. R. Grills, Port lookout on *Aylmer*.

British Warship Losses Ian Allan.

U 333. The Story of a U Boat Ace. Peter Cremer.

U Boat Killer. Captain Donald MacIntyre, DSO, 2 bars, DSC, RN.

Key to map opposite:

HMS *Whittaker*	U 1003
	U 482
HMS *Thane*	U296
MV *Spinanger*	U 1014
MV *Maja*	U 1051
MV *Vignses*	U1024
HMS *Manners*	
MV *Normandy Coast*	
Liberty Ship *Roanoke*	
Two Liferafts	
MV *Galatea*	
MV *Solör*	
Liberty Ship *Ruben Dario*	U 1172
	U1169
U/S Freighter *Jonas Lie*	U 1300
	U 1028
	U1200
Corvette HMS *Vervain*	U 400
	U1063
Liberty Ship *George Hawley*	U 480
	U 1018
	U327
	U 681
	U 683
	U 246
HMS *Teme*	U 1199

The last Naval loss in the area.